70MPH

GRAB THE WHEEL AND HAUL ASS TO YOUR DREAMS

NICK CONEDERA

"This book is a must-read for those of us who wish to experience true freedom and to live our lives in alignment with what matters most. In 70 MPH, Nick shows all of us the fastest way to access the freedom that we all seek."

— Hal Elrod, author,
The Miracle Morning, *www.MiracleMorning.com*

"An epic tale of one brave soul's *Hero's Journey*, this book is equal parts inspiration, motivation and entertainment! A candid glimpse of what life on the road in a van is like, including the challenges and triumphs Nick experienced on his path to rediscovering fulfilment and freedom. My wanderlust has been reinvigorated!"

– Matt Piper,
Vanlifer, www.MauiTheVan.com

"Nick poured his knowledge of living on the road into this book and I'm grateful to know someone who has had the experience of van life to help me better understand and navigate my own journey. To many more adventures."

– Monique Jumonville,
Vanlifer, @thevintagevegans

"Nick Kung-Fu'd his over-achiever lifestyle into a down-to-earth daily adventure. His commentary and instructions for the metamorphosis of van-life are relatable, generous, and vital."

– Kristy Jessica, Vanlifer,
Traveling Muse @_KristyJessica

"As I write this, I'm on week 6 of an epic road trip. No doubt Nick's adventures paved the way for the Vroman family road trip of 2021."

– Jon Vroman,
Front Row Dads @frontrowdads

"Reading this book makes one want to jump in their own van and get *out* and make a life worth living. Whether venturing on the road or safe at home, Nick's story fuels one's soul to truly *live*!"

– Tim Rhode,
1 Life Fully Lived @1lifefullylived

"Everyone knows that Nick is a world-class storyteller. When first opening *70MPH,* I expected to read chapter after chapter of entertaining vanlife stories. Instead, what I experienced was a riveting dose of truth that hit me right between the eyes from the very first chapter. This is one of those books that might just shift your entire life if you're ready for it..."

–Isaac Stegman,
Founder/CEO Kaizen Coaching

Editorial Project Management: Karen Rowe, KarenRowe.com

Editing by: Corey McCullough, *https://www.cbmcediting.com*

Cover Design and Author Image by: Nick Conedera

Interior Layout: Ljiljana Pavkov, pavkovljiljana@gmail.com

Printed in the United States

ISBN: 978-1-63972-239-6 (paperback)

ISBN: 978-1-63972-181-8 (eBook)

"70 MPH ROADMAP"

DRIVING SCHOOL

UPTOWN TOW

REST STOP VILLAGE

CAUTION

BUSINESS DISTRICT & MONEY MANSION

RECOGNITION PEAK

ACHIEVEMENT APEX

PERSONAL GROWTH MOUNTAINS

STOP

PASSION FUEL FACTION

STORY CHURCH

FAMILY FOREST

DOWNTOWN VAN PARTY

NEXT DREAM DESTINATION

To all the wonderful hosts who put me up
and to all the friends I met on the road.

"To know the universe itself as a road, as many roads, as roads for traveling souls."

– *Walt Whitman, "Song for the Open Road*"

TABLE OF CONTENTS

70MPH

INTRODUCTION

Dear Reader,

I read a poem recently that stated that all letters are love letters. Let this be a love letter to you.

I'm not here to tell you what to do with your life. With so many self-proclaimed personal growth gurus and life coaches out there, I find this new fad a little disconcerting. How anybody could believe they have the authority to tell me how to live my life is beyond me. What have *they* done or achieved to deserve such authority?

I have certainly experienced my share of what society tells us is "success" and "happiness." But let me fill you in on a little secret: It's all bullshit.

Real success, happiness, and fulfillment don't come from an external destination. They come from inside.

So what qualifies me to share my story with you? Nothing, really. All I did was burn my old self (literally and figuratively) and take my life on the road. Risky? I'll let you be the judge.

Growing up in sunny San Diego as a surfer, skater, snowboarder, BMX biker, and mountain boarder, I was no stranger to taking risks. Instead of focusing on my grades in high school, I decided to drop all my Honors and AP classes in order to focus full-time on my passion: filmmaking. Before I graduated high school, I had already earned over twenty-five awards for my work, including three student Emmy Awards. I then decided to go against conventional wisdom and get a degree in filmmaking. Meanwhile, in order to raise money for my student films, I sold Cutco Cutlery for a controversial direct-sales program called Vector Marketing and became the top sales rep in the Western Region.

While at film school, I also took a detour to study photography in Italy and ended up traveling through Europe for three months by myself, the experiences of which earned me accolades as an internationally published and international award-winning photographer. And after film school, instead of looking for a job in the film industry, I raised $222,000 from private investors to make my first feature film at only twenty-three years old. A few years later, I started a production company making documentary-style brand films for clients in the personal growth industry that grew into a six-figure business and a feature documentary starring international best-selling author Hal Elrod. I even traveled to Peru to drink ayahuasca with indigenous shamans in the Amazon jungle.

So, here's the big question: What would possess someone with those sorts of credentials to leave his old life behind and live in a van for a year?

Well, after so much "success" as a professional artist, I got bored with the daily grind. Disenchanted, unfulfilled, and lost in a life of nine-to-five production/consumption, I decided to leave my old life behind. At the very height of what others might have considered my "success," I burned my possessions, got rid of my apartment, my car, and my bills, and abandoned my full-time work in order to live in a van and travel the country — to distance myself from organized society in order to remember my true self, connect with my innermost whispers, and realign with my own personal values and priorities. To my surprise, my vanlife lasted longer than a year; it became a permanent lifestyle choice that continues to pay dividends to this day.

Since then, I've come to realize that you can tell a lot about a person by the way they drive. How you drive says a lot about how you go through life. In fact, your car (or, in my case, van) is the perfect metaphor for your life. You are moving through life to some desired destination. And most of us already live so much of our lives in our cars that it's nearly impossible to thrive today without one. So why don't we think more consciously about how we drive through life?

We're all trying to get somewhere. Like a time machine, the faster you move through space, the faster you move through time, and the faster you move through life.

This book is part personal development and part travelogue because, after a couple of years of living on the road in a van, I believe the only way to experience this country —and life in general — is from the road.

The USA is an incredible country. Of course, it's not perfect, but compared to the rest of the world, we have it so good here. The metropolises we've created provide abundance and convenience never before seen in the history of the planet. But that's nothing compared to the sheer natural beauty of this land with its many different types of terrain and natural wonders.

The incredible feat that is the American roadway system is overlooked and underappreciated, but it's one of the wonders of the world. With all our power and money, we've been able to engineer a system that connects the entire country from coast to coast. Millions of miles of black veins crisscross the map, connecting the entire country, bringing food, resources, and commuters to every corner of the nation. And it's available 24/7 to take you wherever you want to go with virtually no limitations except for gas money. It's the perfect metaphor for the universe. Unfortunately, instead of continuing down this boundless road of life, most of us choose to take the exit and get off the "freeway" (the way to freedom) in order to stay in our comfort zone.

This book is about taking the road of life as far as it can go to reach your faraway dream destinations. It includes colorful stories from my own road to Destination Freedom, and I am confident that you'll find value from the growth I experienced, even if it's just as a form of entertainment. Whether you are in love with travel, sick of the nine-to-five rat race, considering the logistics of vanlife for yourself, or simply interested in what I experienced, may this collection of stories from my travels help you to grab the wheel of your own life and haul ass to the destination of your dreams.

Enjoy.

Love,

Nick Conedera

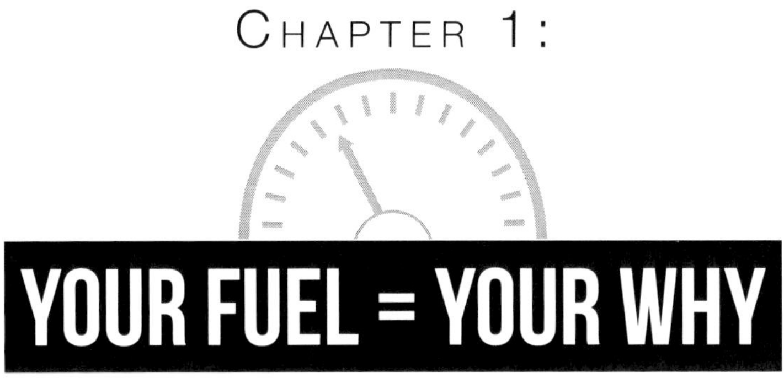

Chapter 1: YOUR FUEL = YOUR WHY

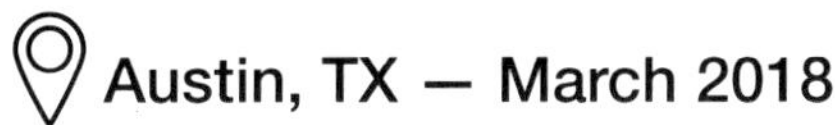

Austin, TX — March 2018

I put the keys in the ignition and sparked the engine.

Vroom-vroom!

And I was off, weaving in and out of traffic, zooming past Priuses and underneath big rigs. While most people were annoyed at being stuck in traffic, I was taking the freeway, going 70 mph.

I had everything you could ever ask for. Six figures, a fast, sexy car, a fancy apartment with four pools, a state-of-the-art gym, and 5.1 surround sound. I traveled constantly. I had a team of video editors working for me. And I had girls (plural).

But… I wasn't happy.

You've heard the story before: The high achiever who has everything decides to throw it all away because no amount of money or trophies or rare art on the walls could fill the black hole in his heart. But why would you ever throw away a perfect life? Because, just like my rally car, I looked sparkly on the outside, but inside, I was a mess — filled with empty beer bottles, discarded junk-food wrappers, smelly gym clothes, and a broken phone charger that I was too lazy to replace.

The truth is, I was lonely and bored with the same routine every day. I hated the work I was doing and was coping with substances, but

I couldn't leave the production/consumption machine I had created because I had to eat. I was locked into a twelve-month lease with bills and a fancy car that required constant upkeep. I felt lost and stuck, broken down on the side of the road with no cell phone or GPS. I didn't even know where I was going.

Then something strange happened.

One day, I was at my local auto parts store when I noticed multiple ambulances coming down the road. I was tired, so I didn't think anything of it.

After my purchase, I went back to the parking lot. That was when I noticed how crowded the lot had become. It was filled to the brim with press, cops, and gridlocked traffic that had been rerouted from the street, which was blocked off by strange-looking cop cars. There was no way out. I was trapped there.

My stomach felt heavy. I knew something was not right.

"What's going on?" I asked one of the guys with press badges.

"Looks like there's been another bombing," he said.

A *bombing*? Was I in some sort of movie? No, this was real. In early 2018, Austin, Texas made national news due to several bombings that occurred at private residences all over the city. Someone had been mailing unmarked packages containing explosive devices to random houses. When the packages were opened by their recipients, they would explode.

I soon learned that earlier that day, a donation box had been dropped off at the Goodwill just down the street from the auto parts store. Inside the box was an incendiary device designed to start a fire. When it was opened, it went off, burning a Goodwill employee, who was taken to the hospital. Luckily, he made a full recovery. This was the seventh and final attack in the box bombing incidents in Austin. The next morning, they caught the guy, who blew himself up before SWAT could arrest him. He was only twenty-three.

Although I was a safe distance from the bomb at the Goodwill that day, the incident affected me.

I felt like I was in a Dalí painting. This stuff *never* happens in real life... Right? I mean, I'd always *heard* about stuff like this, but it never happened in *my* world. Unless, just maybe, I had been living in a bubble which blinded me to the truth.

This realization was a wake-up call for me. It served as an affirmation that there was indeed something wrong with the lifestyle I was living. Perhaps that was why I wasn't happy.

With all the knowledge and resources available to us as a society, how could it be that a twenty-three-year-old could go that far? Unfortunately, the indiscriminate acts of violence in Austin were anything but isolated incidences. The rate of public shootings continues to escalate exponentially. There had already been more shootings in the United States in the first month of 2019 than in an entire year in any other country in the history of the planet. If there are members of our society who are hurting enough to resort to hurting others, then we have some serious soul-searching to do as a species. There must be something broken within our culture.

Psychologists now say that depression is a disease of lifestyle, not a neurological deficiency. In other words, it can be fixed without drugs. With proper exercise, a healthy diet, sunshine, and loved ones, there's not much we can't fix.

I don't believe there is anything wrong with *who* we are; there must be something wrong with what we're *doing* — something about our way of living that is out of alignment with who we are.

But what?

* * *

For hundreds of thousands of years, humans spent the majority of their waking hours on their feet, hunting and gathering in the sunshine, traveling with the seasons, and working together to survive. But our environment and lifestyle have rapidly mutated in just the past few hundred years: putting us inside, by ourselves, on our butts, separating us from nature, feeding us fake food, turning us into human resources.

I believe there's something inherently wrong with how we live today that pushes many of us out of alignment with who we truly are. Perhaps we're not meant to sit on our butts all day. Perhaps we're not meant to live inside boxes all day. Perhaps we're not meant to be so isolated. Perhaps we're not meant to eat this kind of food. Perhaps we're not meant to be chained to one spot. And perhaps we're not meant to work all day, every day.

And what's our reward for all our hard work, anyway? All too often, it's dissatisfaction, a lack of fulfillment, and crippling depression.

In Japan, suicides from being overworked are so common that they have a word for it: *karoshi*. Meanwhile, in the United States, it no longer even surprises us when someone who appears to have it all attempts to take their own life. How is it that so many people whom we consider uber-successful end up committing suicide? Social acceptance seems to come at a deadly price.

In all our years of education, where did we get off at the wrong exit? Shouldn't a lifestyle that drives people to suicide, violence, and murder raise some red flags?

Curious about the Austin box bomber, I did some research. I felt like I knew him somehow. Because although I would have found help for myself before going so far as to kill another human being, I could easily see how, in the wrong environment, facing a difficult set of circumstances, someone could get to that point. There have been several periods in my life when I have felt utterly alone and spiritually lost in my pursuit of personal wealth and achievement to pay for a lifestyle that I didn't even really want. But as a child, that was how I was taught to get not only happiness but also acceptance and love within our social stratification system.

As a talented, educated, ambitious, outgoing young man in Austin, it was easy for me to achieve. I had everything. But I still wasn't happy. I felt like a rat in a maze, racing after the smell of cheese. Only, the maze never ends, and there is no cheese. I was simply doing what everybody else told me to do, living by society's definition of success and happiness rather than defining what that meant for me. But "success" is a moving target, and it was slowly dawning on me that if I kept following this endless path, I would never be fulfilled.

In my opinion, I had contracted the same disease as the serial box bomber. I'd just chosen to deal with my pain in a different way. Instead of hurting others, I distracted myself with alcohol, drugs, sugar, Netflix, painting, travel, hanging with friends… Eventually, I discovered that none of these coping mechanisms cured my spiritual sickness; they only dealt with the symptoms. To heal, I had to change something. And I found myself wondering, *Is it me, or is it my environment?*

Think about it: Why is this the system we've designed for ourselves? Why do we work to pay bills? Why do I need a credit card just to survive? We can and should trust the evolution of billions of humans and thousands of years of civilization, but is this really the best we can do?

As the cost of living rises and average income decreases, it makes less and less sense to me to pay for a lease or a mortgage that puts chains around my neck, shackling me to nothing more than a cage. We're trapped in prisons of our own creation. But it's okay! At least we have all the coffee, sugar, marijuana, alcohol, and Netflix we need to keep us numb to the growing feeling deep down inside that *something just isn't right*.

Our sickness is a spiritual one. Our inner conflict is an existential one. Now that there's no food to hunt, no enemies to fight, no saber-toothed tigers to flee from… who are we? What is our purpose?

I've felt this pain deep down inside, as I'm sure you have at times. It's subtle but enduring, and it doesn't go away. It only gets stronger. But perhaps there is a solution.

Perhaps we are meant for something greater than this.

> This is the story of America. Everybody's doing what they think they're supposed to do.
>
> – *Jack Kerouac, On the Road (1957)*

CHAPTER 2:

YOUR GPS = YOUR HEART

San Diego, CA — December 2017

By the end of 2017, I wasn't even thirty years old, and I had already directed two feature films, traveled all over the world with a camera, lived in Italy, worked with celebrities, won countless awards, earned two degrees, made six figures several years in a row, made videos that went viral to millions of views, wrote a book, spoke on stages in front of thousands, dated models and dancers and actresses, donated time and money to charities, and helped coach other artists to do the same.

In communities all over the country, I was sought after and seen as a leader because I was respected for my work, my talents, and my gumption. It seemed like everybody loved me. People wanted to see me happy and help me succeed. I had reached a point at which anything that I wanted, I got with little or no effort. But there was still something missing deep down inside: an itch that needed to be scratched. *Something*. But I didn't know what. I couldn't put it into words.

I finally reached a breaking point at a client's personal growth event. The event was designed to help attendees manifest their "best year ever." The place was full of overly excited self-employed professionals calling themselves "entrepreneurs," willing to pay good money to hear speakers on stage and connect with other like-minded individuals seeking to grow in their lives and careers.

I had been documenting the event every year since its inception in 2014. It was actually quite wonderful, and to this day, the community is super supportive of each other. But although I felt very at home within the community, that year, I was secretly hoping they'd hire somebody else. I was so burnt out from doing these types of events — over a hundred of them over the previous few years!

I know, I know. "Ugh. They want to pay me all this money to travel to sunny San Diego and do something that I'm really good at and actually enjoy doing." Boo-hoo. Poor me. First-world problems, right?

In retrospect, I think I worked harder on this event than I had on any event I'd ever done before — maybe because this time, I didn't really want to be there. Throughout the course of the entire event, a phrase kept creeping into my mind, almost as if my subconscious was trying to communicate with me. "LIVE IN ALIGNMENT" was the message I kept hearing. But I didn't understand what that meant.

The last speaker on stage wrapped up the final lesson. Everybody in the room was dismissed, confetti fell from the ceiling, fireworks went off, and the attendees left feeling uplifted and ready to change the world while I hid behind the stage and cried.

My engine had finally cracked, and motor oil was leaking into my conscious mind.

* * *

That night, I got drunk and high in my hotel suite with a girl I'd met at the event earlier that day. She was on a high from the event, talking about staying in San Diego a few extra days to hug the palm trees. "I fully support your decision to stay and hug the palm trees," I told her, because that meant more sex to numb the pain. After she left, the loneliness was too much to bear, so I covered up that feeling with more drugs.

I sat at the window in my big fancy suite, overlooking the glittering lights of San Diego bay by myself. I grew up in San Diego, you see. I saw the USS *Midway* aircraft carrier and remembered my senior prom onboard its decks. I saw Coronado Island and thought back to having brunch there with my family many times. I remembered cruising the bay in my dad's sailboat, getting drunk in the Gaslamp with friends, and dancing the night away. I saw a plane landing and thought about how many times I'd flown out of that airport as a kid.

I was so happy as a kid, I thought, *running around with my camera, filming stuff. I was so lucky. I had everything, and what I didn't have, I worked hard to get.*

I wondered what little Nicky would think of me now. I had done more than I'd ever thought possible. Yet here I was, feeling like I was at rock bottom.

That was when I had a vision.

As I looked out on San Diego from my hotel room, a massive object suddenly rose from the streets below to hover just outside my window — like the upgraded DeLorean time machine from *Back to the Future Part II*.

It was a big white van.

To be clear, this was no luxury vehicle (to be honest, it looked more like the kind of thing a mom would report to the police if she saw it lingering near a playground). The floating van seemed to look at me with its big headlights, straight into my soul, like it knew me. The driver's door opened, inviting me inside. Then the engine hood opened like a mouth, and it spoke to me.

"It's time to go," it said.

"Where are we going?" I asked.

"Destination Freedom."

With that, it flew off into the night like a spaceship, disappearing into the stars.

Well, that was weird…

I slept like a baby that night. The next morning, I began my morning routine by heating up some water for tea with the coffee maker, giving it a little bit of that burnt coffee taste that I had grown to love. Back then, I traveled so much that hotels had become home to me (even more so than my fancy apartment), so I brought everything with me, including my Yogi Tea. I love my Yogi Tea because every tea bag comes with a fortune printed on the tag. "Use your head to live with heart," was the wisdom from my Yogi Tea bag that morning.

I stopped. I knew immediately that this wise little tea bag was right. I was ignoring my heart. I was not — to use the words that had seemingly pursued me throughout the recent seminar — *living in alignment*.

There were so many things that I wanted to do but was putting off because I thought I was supposed to be making money and building my business. My mind wasn't in alignment with my heart. In fact, they were usually in conflict. This, I have since learned, can lead to countless uh-ohs, like discomfort, unfulfillment, a sense of being lost, loneliness, pain, disease, and even trauma. I was listening to other people's definitions of success and happiness rather than listening to my own heart. How is it that what we're told to do could be in such contention with the wisdom of our souls?

It was time to start taking myself more seriously. It was time to love and respect myself enough to live in alignment with my heart's desires: what I truly wanted in life.

This explained the visit from that white pedophile van. I'd always wanted to unplug from civilization and spend my time free from schedules and bills and obligations to just travel the country in a van. To just say, "FUCK IT!" And live free. It had been on my vision boards for years. I was about to turn thirty and wasn't tied down by a family or another project.

If I was ever going to do it, now was the time.

Choosing to live in alignment is the highest expression of self-love because it puts you on the road that leads directly to your happiness, your fulfillment, your dream destination.

To live in alignment means to align your heart (or soul or spirit) with your mind and body. Whatever it is that sets your heart on fire — your dreams, your passions, your visions, your bliss, your INSPIRATION — this is your North Star. It's the magic compass that directs you where to go. The GPS that guides you.

You must use your mind's eye to strategize and ENVISION how to get to your destination, then use your body to put it into ACTION. Why else would you have these feelings and desires? *Because you are supposed to pursue them.*

Chapter 3:

YOUR ROADMAP

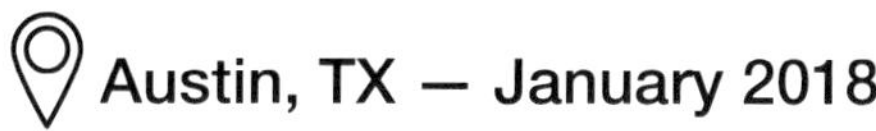

Austin, TX — January 2018

I spent hours and hours looking at vans on Craigslist.

This is crazy, right? Not crazy like the palm tree hugger in my hotel room, but another kind of crazy. (To clarify, there's nothing wrong with hugging palm trees.) I was being called to get rid of my nice life — most everybody's definition of success and happiness — to live in a van down by the river. And in the end, the call didn't come from an $80,000 Mercedes Sprinter with a slick interior. It came from an old white cargo van, the kind used most often by day laborers or plumbers. If this wasn't crazy, then what was?

> Here's to the crazy ones, the misfits, the rebels, the troublemakers, the round pegs in the square holes... the ones who see things differently. They're not fond of rules... You can quote them, disagree with them, glorify or vilify them, but the only thing you can't do is ignore them because they change things... they push the human race forward, and while some may see them as the crazy ones, we see genius, because the ones who are crazy enough to think that they can change the world, are the ones who do.
>
> —*Steve Jobs*

I made good money, so I was used to a cushy life. How was I supposed to live in a dirty old van that looked like it should have had "Free Candy" painted on the side? I had no idea what I was doing or where I was going. But the vision continued to pull me like a moth to a flame. Was I going to fry in the fires of the brilliant white light?

I was also super anal about most things. "OCD" was a phrase I used to barely cover up the truth that I was a control freak. I loved organizing shit, planning, and making lists. (I remember reading somewhere that "successful people think on paper," and I had chosen to believe it.) So naturally, I had a seven-part roadmap for my van adventure.

MY 2018 #VANLIFE ROADMAP

Phase 1: Get rid of my possessions — liquidate all electronics and equipment, throw away that which can't be salvaged, donate all furniture and houseware, and burn the rest.

Phase 2: Shop for vans, test-driving at least a dozen.

Phase 3: Trade in my lovely sports car for a shitty van.

Phase 4: Stop working (which meant no income).

Phase 5: Build a house inside the van (even though I had no construction experience).

Phase 6: Break my lease (which would surely be expensive).

Phase 7: Travel around for a year like a vagabond.

And if it didn't go exactly according to plan, I knew I'd be distraught!

* * *

At this point, I'd like to step away from the story for a moment and share some of the insights I've gained in the years between then and now. Because while my #VANLIFE roadmap might seem overly meticulous to some, maybe even unnecessary, I've learned that one of the secrets to manifestation is CLARITY.

Planning a roadmap like this for any personal or professional endeavor will always bring added clarity to your plan. It makes your vision sharper and more focused, and therefore, it is easier to articulate specific actions and tasks — in other words, HOW to make it happen by breaking down the process. A little planning might even help clarify WHY you're doing it, too! (Insert *Hallelujah Chorus* here.)

Thanks to my obsessive planning methods, I was able to budget the entire van project pretty succinctly in terms of both time and money. The results? I would finish the project right at budget with only a few cosmetic things I couldn't afford, and right on time (I was sweeping the sawdust out of my new van home the day before I left on my maiden voyage, but more on that later).

Planning is a very important part of your journey because you can't get to your dream destinations without (a) a roadmap or (b) breaking down your big destination into smaller, achievable steps. Making a plan puts you in the driver's seat, as opposed to "winging it" and throwing caution to the wind.

And so, after test-driving about a dozen vans, I had a clear idea of what my options were:

- $80,000 Mercedes Sprinter, fully loaded
- $15,000–$25,000 blank canvas
- $10,000 cargo van

Some of the vehicles on my list weren't even in working condition. Others were already fully prepared for the vanlife. Diesel. Gas. New. Old. I even looked at a 24-passenger bus.

No matter what I chose, I was planning on doing the interior build myself, so I went to check out one last cargo van, just like the one I had seen in my vision. It was at one of those used car lots in the middle of nowhere. Except this used car lot… wasn't really a lot. It was just a house with a dirt yard and a bunch of cars parked around it.

The owner, a Middle Eastern guy, had three white cargo vans to look at. They seemed to be in pretty good condition. He left me alone to peruse in private. Being overly obsessed with planning, I went into my pocket to get my phone so I could check my van list, and

I dropped my chapstick on the ground. When I bent down to grab it, I was at eye level with one of the vans. And it smiled at me.

Now, I'm *pretty* sure I'm not schizophrenic. Maybe a little crazy, but I don't hallucinate in broad daylight on a regular Thursday without some sort of drug in me. But my connection to this van was palpable. I could feel it. Literally smiling at me. It was as if my presence turned it on, and it said, "HELLO! I like you."

This was not the van I had come here to see. Instead, it was an older Ford Econoline E350 Super Duty 5L Cargo Van that was more run-down than the rest. It also had over 100,000 miles on it already. But, for whatever reason, this van and I had a connection. I remember thinking right away, *I think this is the one.*

Just to be safe, I took it to a mechanic nearby to get a full inspection. Despite the mileage, the engine was in perfect condition, which was more important to me than its aesthetic. The mechanic was actually weirded out. "I've never seen an old work vehicle in this condition," he told me. "They took really good care of this van."

So I gave the Middle Eastern guy my car and wrote a check for $4,000, and the van was mine.

Chapter 4:

YOUR CARGO = YOUR POSSESSIONS

Austin, TX — January 2018

> My greatest skill has been to want little.
>
> —*Henry David Thoreau, Walden (1854)*

I lit a match and threw it on my most prestigious Emmy award. It was soaked in lighter fluid, so it erupted immediately into a big ball of flame. I watched as the name *Nick Conedera*, printed on the award, slowly disintegrated into black nothingness.

It was my third and most coveted Emmy award, which I'd won in high school for a short film called *Melvin* (2006), a coming-of-age story about a boy who adopts and loses a pet snail he named Melvin. *Melvin* was the first major production that I did on my own, outside of school. I wrote the script, storyboarded the shots, cast one of my best friends, shot the film, edited it, chose the music, and even did the titles myself.

Melvin was charming, adorable, fun, meaningful, and poignant — the perfect blend of entertainment and substance. A near-perfect short film. It received recognition at every festival and competition in San Diego, garnering about half a dozen laurels and awards. And because my first major attempt at telling my own stories had been so wildly successful with such a simple short film, the award was a very meaningful award to me. The object itself gave me a sense of significance and knowledge that I was good at something — that I was worth something, that my life had meaning.

And just like that, it was gone.

By age thirty, I had become so attached to the identity of being a talented and decorated filmmaker. Without that identity… who was I?

For a second, I feared that seeing my name fade into oblivion meant that I was fading into oblivion myself. But once the flames transmuted my attachment into a pile of carbon, I felt a weight lift. I felt lighter. And it became easier. So I followed suit with the rest of my awards. Thirty or so trophies and certificates — chunks of glass and plastic that I had been carrying around for over a decade to prove my worth to the world — slowly melted and combusted into black nothingness.

Right from the beginning, I knew that part of the process of preparing for the minimalism of vanlife would mean getting rid of my possessions. I decided that the van had to be able to contain my entire life, including clothes, toiletries, kitchen stuff, food, water, important documents, and the film equipment that allowed me to make a living.

Fortunately, I'm not a very material person. In fact, I hate Christmas. But getting rid of certain objects was still really hard for me. The things I found myself most attached to included art that I never displayed, old journals that I never read, yearbooks that I never opened, and film equipment that I never used. Much of this was stuff that I continued to hang on to only because I felt so attached to it.

But the awards were especially meaningful to me. Somewhere along the way, I had learned how to gain attention through achievement and recognition. And because of the way our social stratification system is set up, I think we sometimes confuse attention with love. We gain social status, acceptance, and power from success/achievement. So, no matter where I lived, I always made sure my trophies were the first thing you saw when you entered my home. But other than a moment of my ego's shameless pleasure when I noticed somebody's silent awe of my trophy case, the physical awards gave me no value.

It dawned on me that I was attached to the identity and the good feelings of nostalgia that these things gave me, not the items themselves. But by being attached to them, they became part of me. Those journals *are* me, those awards *are* me, those yearbooks, those cameras… How could I get rid of a piece of myself? Imagine getting rid of your hand or your ear or your liver.

Not surprisingly, the more I did it, the easier it got. And eventually, I was able to get rid of everything that was not directly contributing to my survival. I sold all my electronics and equipment on Craigslist. I donated or gifted all my furniture. And I burned the rest.

Okay, I'll admit, I did keep *some* art, books, and family photos that are still in storage. And my dad wouldn't let me get rid of my camera collection because I'd inherited much of it from my grandfather. So there were a few items important enough to keep in the family. But other than that, only the essentials.

* * *

To be clear, shedding your material possessions doesn't mean a mass-purge of every item you own. You don't want to do something drastic that you'll regret later, so it is okay to keep some of the things that really matter to you.

You may have heard of the book *The Life-Changing Magic of Tidying Up* by Marie Kondo. In it, she suggests that you hold each object close to your heart to feel its energy. If it doesn't make you feel good or add value to your life, put it in the discard pile. It always sounded so cheesy to me, but it wasn't until I watched the documentary *Minimalism* (2015) that it really began to make sense.

All the stuff you own ends up owning you because of an invisible energetic tie you have to it. And there's something magical that happens when you cleanse your life of physical objects and break free of those unhealthy attachments. Once I got rid of it all, my life was simpler and less cluttered. I really did feel lighter, and I was noticeably happier. Strange, I know. I would never have guessed.

I discovered that the more objects I purged from my life, the more room there was for newer/better things to enter. And I'm not just talking about material possessions — there was now room for greater clarity and new ideas, opportunities, and relationships.

These material possessions had served a purpose. But it was time to stop clinging to them. Time for me to replace society's superficial acceptance with true self-love, giving myself the love I knew I deserved not because of what I'd done, but because of who I was inside.

The more love you give yourself, the more you will receive — from me and from everybody else.

How much cargo are you hauling?

The less you have, the lighter you are, the more aerodynamic you are, and the easier and quicker you can move through life. Some of your destinations may require that you travel lighter, and you can't make it up that mountain if you're weighed down by a bunch of useless crap. So get rid of your shit! You may be surprised how much mental energy it frees up, leaving room for newer and better things.

CHAPTER 5:

YOU ARE THE FACTORY

Austin, TX — February 2018

"Do you have any idea how loud you're being?"

I paused from my work and turned around to find a super friendly neighbor standing there. He was trying his best to be mean and scary, but it just wasn't working.

"Umm, yes I do," I replied honestly. "I'm cutting wood. Sorry. It's loud."

In fact, I probably knew better than anybody else how loud it was, considering the circular saw was spinning right in front of my face.

"I'm trying to read," he fumed.

I didn't know how to respond to this. Of course, his goal was to get me to be quiet, which could have been easily accomplished by politely asking how long I would be working. But instead, he vomited his feelings at me. So I simply replied, "Have you tried headphones?"

Then there was a long, awkward silence.

"You can't do that here…" he said. "It's rude to everybody who lives here. Do you even care?"

I strongly disagreed with him on all these fronts, but it was clear that there'd be no compromising with this guy. So instead of being rude right back to him, I simply tried to acknowledge his feelings.

There was no way I was going to stop building the interior of my new van just because of his annoyance.

Admittedly, I wasn't a resident in this neighborhood. My buddy was letting me use his garage and tools to build the interior of my newly purchased van. But we weren't breaking any of the apartment complex's rules, nor was I breaking any laws. I was doing my construction within the allotted timeframe that they had given us (9 a.m. to 5 p.m.) during the day, when residents were usually gone at work. I'm sure this man could have called the police on me if he'd wanted to, but it would have accomplished nothing other than pissing off a cop with much better things to do.

"Of course I care," I said. "I understand. I get annoyed with loud noises, too. I just choose to either not let it bother me or use some headphones or earplugs. So what can I do for you?"

"Well..." he said. "This is a neighborhood, not a construction zone. You need to do this someplace else."

Now, I consider myself a reasonable person, and I like to help people. But this guy just wanted to hate me for what I was doing, and he wanted to ensure that I fully comprehended just *how* much he hated me for messing up his day.

"I'd like to help," I said, "but I'm not going to move my whole production just for you. Sorry again."

"So you're just an asshole, then."

"I guess so," I replied kindly.

No need to argue there.

I guess he ran out of insults at that point because he slithered away, steaming.

I continued to do my building at that location for another couple of months, and the guy never bothered me again. I did, however, get a couple more noise complaints. Obstacles are inevitable, and this was just one of the many obstacles I ran into when deciding to turn a van into a home, all on my own.

* * *

D.I.Y. is constant problem-solving, and I love to solve problems.

Because I'm a very hands-on kind of guy, I wouldn't have enjoyed saving up for an $80,000 Sprinter or $50,000 Sportsmobile that was already built out. I didn't have a ton of money, but I did have the time and determination to do it myself.

To me, this van was more than just a fun project; it was my opportunity to take my life into my own hands. I was redesigning myself and, therefore, my life. The van itself was a symbol of my freedom. I wanted to learn. I wanted to have fun. I wanted to put my own sweat and blood and tears into the project to ensure that I was completely invested and serious about this major life change I was about to make. These are the perfect conditions for "do it yourself."

In reality, you can do a project like this two of three ways: cheap, fast, or easy. Not all three. Cheap and fast means super complicated. Fast and easy translates to expensive. And then there's easy and cheap, which means it will take you a long time. I chose to do it fast and cheap and to do it myself (which, as it turned out, was not easy).

It took me about ten weeks to finish the van, which is pretty fast considering I had limited construction experience. It cost me about $12,500 (including the sticker price of the van), which is pretty cheap. But my life was consumed by this project for those three months. I became a construction worker, building seven days a week, three to twelve hours a day. I took only a few days off due to weather or because of construction problems that I simply had to wait to do. It was physically painful and exhausting but so rewarding. I found pleasure in the work unlike anything I'd felt before.

Step by step, here's how I built the van…

1.) Research

I studied how others did their van builds.
Tools: Google, internet

2.) Design

I made blueprints and drawings for the build.
Tools: My brain, paper and pencil, hand drawings, spreadsheets, etc.

3.) Repairs

I made repairs to the engine, brakes, electrical system, and air vents.

Tools: I hired local mechanics, costing big $$$

4.) Demolition

I gutted what was already in the van.

Tools: Hammer, rubber mallet, pick, screwdriver, angle grinder, screw gun

5.) Cleaning/Prep

I prepared the body of the van for construction, which included cleaning, removing rust, and more cleaning!

Tools: Angle grinder, vacuum, hose, cleaning supplies

6.) Painting

I had to paint and seal the interior before construction could begin.

Supplies: White Glossy Rustoleum spray for Auto

7.) Insulation

I used four different types of insulation for the walls, ceiling, floor, and little nooks/crannies.

Supplies: Foam insulation, Pink Panther fiberglass, Reflectix, spray foam

Tools: Knife, epoxy, spray adhesive, gloves, mask

8.) Paneling

I paneled the walls and ceiling for looks and protection.

Supplies: Lauan, Reflectix, spray adhesive

Tools: Screw gun, screws

9.) Paneling the doors

I decided to panel the doors, too, just for fun!

Supplies: Maps from old Thomas Guide, lauan, wheat paste, polyurethane

Tools: Paint brushes, screw gun, screws

10.) Flooring

Every home needs a floor!

Supplies: I chose plywood with one-by-three supports and foam insulation, then vinyl pasted on top with special vinyl adhesive and caulk
Tools: Screw gun and screws, spray adhesive, rollers

11.) The Build
Construction and carpentry.
Supplies: Lots of wood, one-by-threes, two-by-fours, plywood of all kinds, carpet, spray adhesive
Tools: Skilsaw, router saw, miter saw, electric sander, tape measure, gloves, eye protection, hammer, screw gun, screws, hand drill and bits, wrenches, ratchets (pretty much every tool you can think of)

12.) Electronics
For the electrical system, I needed a battery system, a new stereo, new speakers, a backup camera, LED lighting, a vent with an electric fan, and solar panels. My buddy Matt did all the electrical work and wiring for me.
Supplies: Wiring, speaker wire, switches
Tools: Ohmmeter, wire cutter and stripper, knife, needle nose pliers, screw gun, screws

13.) HVAC
Heating, A/C, and ventilation.
Supplies: Regular ducting and special duct tape, "RV vent fan 2000," plus wiring
Tools: Screw gun, screws, angle grinder to cut a hole in the roof, wiring tools

14.) Cabinetry
So I can store stuff securely!
Supplies: Prefab cabinets from Home Depot (or else it would have taken forever)
Tools: Tape measure, screw gun, screws, epoxy

15.) Water System
I chose a hand pump with a two-tank system: a freshwater tank and a gray water tank.

Supplies: Waterproof caulk, hand pump, bundt cake bake pan as the sink, rubber tubing, six-gallon tank, three-gallon tank
Tools: Screw gun, screws, miter saw

16.) Refrigeration System
Depending on your power supply, this can be tricky. I didn't have enough power to run something like a refrigerator, so I chose a cooler system.
Supplies: Insulated water cooler, ice
Tools: None (I kept it simple)

17.) Painting/Finishing
For this step, I had to decide whether I wanted to keep the white pedophile van look. I didn't… but I ran out of time and money. I did, however, paint the grill and all the trim with truck bed liner.
Supplies: Rhino Paint truck bed liner, spray gun
Tools: Rented air compressor from Home Depot, air hose, gasoline

18.) Bells and Whistles
Finishing touches.
Supplies: Swivel seat, camper top storage, steering wheel cover, butt cushion, decor, magnets, etc.

19.) Curtains and Cushions
For privacy, comfort, and insulating the windows. My Mom sewed all these for me. Thanks, Mom!
Supplies: Fabrics, mylar, high-powered neodymium magnets, thread, polyester fiber
Tools: Sewing machine, needles, thimble, pins

20.) Bed
I kept my old Ikea foam mattress (very nice and comfortable). These are made in square grids that are very easy to cut with a knife, so I was able to cut it to the exact size for the back of the van.
Supplies: Foam mattress, sheets, pillows, blankets
Tools: Knife

21.) Kitchen

I kept it simple and mobile with a Coleman camping stove.
Supplies: Propane stove, propane canister, hoses, pots, pans, knives, cutting board, plates, utensils, spices, cups, etc.
Tools: None (I kept it simple)

22.) TEST!

My maiden voyage was camping in Moab, UT in order to test the entire system. Then I came back to Austin to make adjustments.

* * *

At first glance, this process might look pretty intimidating to a beginner, but keep in mind that I was a total beginner, too. And since I had so little experience in construction, a lot of my time was spent in Step 1, the research phase. I had to learn how to do pretty much everything myself.

I'd like to thank the internet, without which this project would probably not have been possible. I'd also like to thank a few organizations that proved invaluable. Like Home Depot, which was the only reason I could build so quickly (sometimes I was at Home Depot three times a day!). I'd like to thank Amazon, which provided every single custom part and appliance I needed for the van. Thanks to Chipotle, which fed me constantly. And to Starbucks, which got me up in the morning.

And I'd also like to thank my buddy Matt, who let me take over his garage and all his tools (and annoy his neighbors) for those three months. I don't know if the skills I developed will ever be useful to me again, but I learned a ton, and it was so much fun.

On the road of life, you are the vehicle. The challenge is that you are also the factory.

You are the designer, you are the engineer, you are the CEO, and you are the laborers in manufacturing.

The bottom line: You are your own creator. You are the masterpiece of your own life. You are Michelangelo, and the David you are sculpting is YOU. So if something in your

> **life goes wrong, who's to blame? Nobody's going to take responsibility for you. If something breaks, nobody's there to fix it but you.**

Nothing ever goes perfectly. In the case of my van, I'm proud of what I accomplished, but there was still a lot I wasn't able to accomplish within my allotted timeframe and budget (like my plans for the locks, alarm system, bug shield, exterior painting, ladder, bike rack, bullbar and grill guard, fender flares, muffler, 4×4 conversion, lift kit, etc.). Not to mention that a bunch of stuff broke, including a door panel and the instrument panel. At one point, we drilled through an A/C line, broke the stereo and had to get a new one, broke the lights and had to get replacements, lost a hub cap somewhere along the road… But these speedbumps are what make the journey fun.

Once I was finished, I had to name the van. I dubbed him Janüs after the ancient Roman god of new beginnings and endings, transitions, doorways, pathways, travel, and commerce. The perfect name. Janüs was to be the vehicle for my transition into a new life and a new me.

Chapter 6:

YOUR STEERING WHEEL = YOUR CHOICES AND ACTIONS

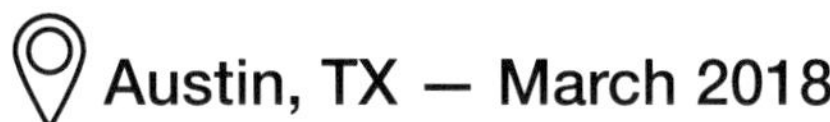

Austin, TX — March 2018

Ten weeks of building, and I was ready for my freedom.

After completing the van's finishing touches, it was time to depart. Just in time, too. I finished the van, cleaned out all the sawdust, and moved in with all my stuff the day before I set off on my first trip.

That same day, I also rented a U-Haul and took my remaining furniture to Goodwill. And that night, I slept on the floor of my empty apartment, which was kind of surreal. The morning of my departure, I cut my mattress to fit in the back of the van, left my apartment keys at the leasing office, and left.

As I turned the key in the ignition, a strange feeling came over me. I had prepared for this moment for months. But the expected elation was absent. Instead, I found myself thinking more about the discomfort I was about to endure.

I had spent enough time traveling to know how uncomfortable it can be, especially when you don't have a home. I'd put so much time and effort — not to mention all my money — into creating this new lifestyle, and I had just gotten rid of all my possessions and my apartment. Was I crazy? Was it going to be worth it? Was I going to hate it? Would I have enough money?

For a second, I was terrified. Frightened of the unknown. But then I remembered that this was how I *preferred* to live: on the edge of the unknown, surfing the interface between calculated control and complete chaos. Living life at 70 mph.

I adjusted the rearview mirror, put the van into gear, and hit the gas.

Next stop: DESTINATION FREEDOM! A magical place where all your dreams come true.

But wait a minute... I thought as the wheels started rolling. *Where* is *"Destination Freedom"? And how do I get there?*

Hmm... I have no idea. Guess I'll figure it out along the way.

Onward!

* * *

Hindsight is always 20/20. But when you're in the moment, you can never foresee the waves of change that will result from your individual choices. I certainly didn't know that my life was about to change dramatically, nor that *I* was about to change dramatically. And I couldn't have possibly understood how that change would affect everybody around me — all the people I met on the road, all the friends I visited, and all the family who witnessed my change.

One degree of separation puts the ship miles off its original course. I made waves in the space-time continuum because I had unwittingly forced myself miles out of my comfort zone. And so, in addition to the effects I'm aware of, there are probably many things that happened as a direct result of my decision to live in a van that I will never know about.

There was no stopping what I had set in motion. The snowball was already too massive and had too much momentum. I gave myself no alternative routes. The only way out was to grab the bull by the balls and hang on for dear life.

Only you decide which direction to go. You control your direction with your metaphorical steering wheel. The question is, where are you headed? And is it where you really *want* to be going?

Are you charting a course toward "Marriage Mountains" to create a family, or "Violin Valley" to be a musician? Or maybe you're trying to reach "Oratory Ocean" to become a speaker. Wherever it is that you're heading, remember that it's your hands on the wheel. And how do you take the first step toward the life of your dreams? You make a decision and put it into action.

Your decisions and actions determine your course. But it's usually not just one big decision that changes everything. It's the conglomeration of all those small, seemingly insignificant decisions you make on a daily basis. Those micro-adjustments of the steering wheel might change your direction by a fraction of a degree, but a year later, you're miles away from where you would have been. Each day you decide not to exercise may push you closer and closer to "Depression Drive." Every dollar you save today may be one less mile to "Comfort Cavern" when you finally retire. Each and every decision you make creates waves in the space-time continuum that ripple out to affect not only your life but the lives of everybody around you.

There is no way to predict what may manifest as a result of your decisions. You are surfing the wave of space-time, hanging ten on the crest between the past and the future.

So, where do you want to steer your vehicle?

DETOUR #1

Butte, MT

Every trip has its share of detours, and before we continue along the road of my story, I'd like to offer a fun detour by sharing one of my favorite destinations.

One of the most romantic aspects of the vanlife is obviously the opportunity to travel. While in the van, I traveled through 40 states, and in my opinion, life on the road is the best way to see the country because you truly get to experience it.

The US is a beautiful country and should be cherished, not disparaged. It's incredible how many worlds there can be in one country — so many nooks and crannies filled with their own experiences, people, history, colors, food, culture, feeling, and energy. Places are as diverse as people, and I'd like to share with you some of the most interesting locations I've experienced. Hopefully these sections will seduce you to fall in love with our country all over again and maybe even inspire you to do your own traveling.

Here's to celebrating the beautiful diversity that is the United States of America.

* * *

When you learn about the Second Industrial Revolution, you'll often hear about Carnegie's steel, Vanderbilt's railroads, J.P. Morgan's banks, Rockefeller's oil, Henry Ford's horseless carriage, and, of course, the war of the currents between Thomas Edison's DC (backed by J.P. Morgan) and Nikola Tesla's AC (backed by Westinghouse). But for some reason, you don't learn about copper.

Without copper, electrical power for the consumer marketplace would have been a non-starter. As our dependence on oil-based lanterns diminished, millions of miles of copper wiring were needed to light a newly electrified America. And where did all that copper come from? Butte, Montana.

At one point, Butte was producing two-thirds of all the copper in the world and 99 percent of the copper in the US. If your house was built before 1980, chances are you have electric wiring made from copper that came from Butte.

At one point, the city was bigger and wealthier than San Francisco, with a population of over 100,000. But today, most of the copper production is automated, and most of the mines are shut down, leaving the bedrock below Butte like Swiss cheese, with 10,000 miles of empty channels. And with a population of only 30,000, most of the buildings are now abandoned or unused, leaving the city frozen in time. It's like stepping out of a time machine.

Upon arriving, I was directed by some locals to a former brothel, newly converted into a Chinese restaurant. The private booths that had once been used for legal copulation were now private dining areas, hidden by discreet red curtains. To be honest, I felt claustrophobic. The booths were very small, but I guess just big enough for… all kinds of opium-induced pleasures. The food was less than great.

Later, I met my hosts at their distillery, where I learned that their main business was manufacturing high-quality upright stills, although they also owned a distillery of their own, producing all kinds of popular high-quality spirits. They took me out to a fancy steak restaurant and showered me with champagne in the hot tub, and the next day, we went around the city, checking out all the old buildings, the mines, and digging into the history of the place.

I've always been fascinated by the Second Industrial Revolution and have always wanted to make a film set during that era. But I'd never heard anything about copper. Why? Why do all the studies of this period neglect the story of copper? This inquiry inspired a deep dive into the history of the town and the copper mining that made it so famous.

* * *

At the end of a long day of exploring the history and mines of Butte, we all went to my hosts' manufacturing facility, located on top of one of the main mines, the Anaconda. I got to see how they produce high-quality stills for distilleries all over the world. And at the back of their property, there's an overlook that oversees the Berkeley Pit.

The Berkeley Pit is a giant depression in the earth, a mile wide, now filled with acidic groundwater containing toxic byproducts of copper production. The toxic turquoise liquid has an incredibly acidic pH of 2.5 — strong enough to dissolve the steel propeller of a boat. Back in 2016, a flurry of 10,000 migrating geese landed in the pond to rest for the night. Thousands died. Hundreds more were found dead in the surrounding areas, up to ten miles away. The town smelled like death for months.

As we were talking about this pit, a small private jet flew over us and landed on an airstrip somewhere among the thousands of acres owned by the mining company that still operates there. It was probably the CEO. Who else would be flying into a tiny town in a private jet? I couldn't help but wonder what this place looked like from overhead, and what it had looked like before the mining industry, back when it was still an unspoiled natural wonder.

It seems that stories of incredible change and revolution always end with personal, social, or environmental failures in the wake of tremendous financial gains. So is revolution worth it?

The byproducts of change are many — some good, some bad. We destroyed a beautiful place in the mountains of Montana, but we electrified the country by doing so. One thing's for certain: it's a fascinating story of the history of our country. And I might never have known if not for a small detour I took.

Make sure you make enough time for some detours.

You never know what you'll discover. Whether it's driving drunk in a hijacked golf cart on the Warner Bros backlot in the middle of the night, flying in a Cessna with a hesitant new pilot over McAllen, Texas, drinking ayahuasca with indigenous shamans in Peru, or sipping margaritas on the sharp lava rocks of Hawaii... Detours always lead to experiences, stories, lessons, and opportunities.

CHAPTER 7:

YOUR RADIO = YOUR THOUGHTS AND EMOTIONS

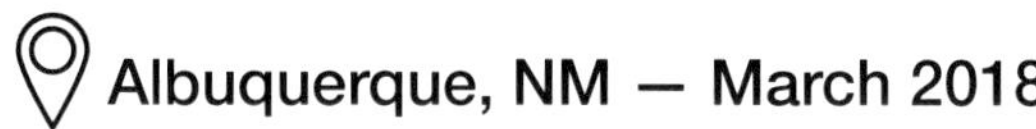

Albuquerque, NM — March 2018

I was finally on the road. Me and Janüs on the maiden voyage to Moab, Utah, caravanning with my buddy Matt and his girlfriend for Jeep Week. And was it everything I had hoped it would be?

No. It sucked.

I hadn't driven the van much on the freeway yet, so hours and hours on the highways soon exposed the consequence of having no cruise control. It also revealed that the van was super difficult to control because of its boxy shape. Very squirrelly. I just couldn't keep it in a straight line. I kept thinking, *There must be something wrong with the alignment or tie rods or something*. When I stopped for gas, I realized that it was super windy, and that may have been contributing to the problem.

But it didn't stop there.

My buddy Matt wanted to get to Albuquerque by the end of the first day, but that meant a long day of driving. Twelve hours, to be exact. So by the end of the day, I was deliriously tired and in great pain from sitting for so long. Luckily, all I had to do was crawl into the back of the van to go to sleep.

Day 2 was no better…

I was enjoying some tunes accompanying the visuals of the natural beauty of New Mexico when little white specks started falling from the sky.

Is that… snow? In the desert? In the Spring?

Yes. We'd hit a freak ice storm, and soon, it was a full-blown blizzard. I could barely see thirty feet in front of me. The snow was so thick on the road that people were pulling off to the side to wait it out (hopefully by choice).

My imagination went wild. Here I was, my first trip in this vehicle that was a three-month labor of love, and the likelihood that I would crash on my maiden voyage suddenly seemed fairly high. But I had to keep going, slowly but surely, slipping and sliding, white-knuckling it the whole way.

* * *

After a couple of hours driving at about twenty miles an hour through blizzard conditions, we finally made it out of the storm zone and stopped for gas and lunch. I'd been completely unprepared for snow, but Janüs had handled it like a champ. I felt like a proud daddy. What a crazy start to my van adventure!

There were only a few hours left between us and Moab. But my mind was racing. What else was going to go wrong? These things happen in threes, right? What if I got a flat tire? What if the van broke down in the middle of nowhere? What had I been thinking, doing this stupid van thing? I wasn't prepared at all — oy vey!

At that point, I finally noticed the game my mind was playing with my thoughts and emotions, so I slammed on the (metaphorical) brakes.

If you are your vehicle, and your engine is your mind, then the music you play while driving represents your thoughts and emotions. Thoughts and emotions influence each other, and too much thinking in one direction creates emotions in your body. These thereby give birth to new thoughts that match that emotional tone or feeling. It's a feedback loop that's easy to get stuck in.

A good way to break this cycle: Change the channel on the radio.

A good way for me to change the channel in my mind is to listen to podcasts. For some reason, the chatter of dialogue puts my mind at ease. So I turned on Joe Rogan to listen to him smoke weed with Elon Musk and talk about AI and electric cars. A change of station disrupted the pattern and broke me out of the negative cycle.

Of course, I'm speaking figuratively, but music is also a great way to influence and control your mood, which gives you the power to manage your thoughts and emotions. What do you like to listen to while driving? Podcasts, audiobooks, heavy metal, 90s, jazz, classical, or relaxing meditation music? Do you like to learn, or to rock out? Do you like to let your mind drift or focus on something specific?

The thing about a (literal) radio is that you're in control. You choose what to play. You choose the channel, and you choose when to press play and stop. We often forget that we have the same control of our thoughts and emotions.

You are not your thoughts — they're just electric impulses in your brain, and they have no control over you. You are not your emotions, either — they're just chemicals in your body, and they have no control over you. But that doesn't mean you should ignore them completely. Your thoughts and emotions are part of a very intelligent guidance system, and they are valuable communicators. But your job is to use your conscious mind to understand what it is your thoughts and emotions are trying to communicate to you. Are you simply afraid of something happening because it has happened in the past? That doesn't necessarily mean it will happen again. You're taking a wrong turn if you're allowing your thoughts and emotions to dictate your decisions and actions.

An inauspicious start to my journey had nearly shaken my resolve. But I changed the channel in my mind that day and tuned in to a different station. One that served me well.

Finally, we arrived at our campsite in Moab. Although I was tired, I was in a good mood because I was no longer allowing my mind to control my thought patterns. And the best part: Nothing bad happened. It was all in my head, after all.

> The wolf that wins is the one you feed.
>
> —*Cherokee proverb*

CHAPTER 8:

DRIVER'S ED

Moab, UT — March 2018

"You're acting like a fucking ninny," the emergency room doctor scolded me.

I was doubled over, holding my side in great pain, and the doctor at Moab Regional Hospital was... *cursing* at me? I thought this van thing was going to be fun!

So how the heck did I get here? Let's rewind...

After a long two days of driving, we'd finally reached our campsite in Moab. Matt set up his backpacking stove and heated up some gluten-free/dairy-free mac 'n' cheese. It was so good, especially around a cozy campfire underneath the stars! The cheese substitute was nutritional yeast. So delicious. I ate a lot... Maybe too much.

In the middle of the night, I woke up feeling really strange. I felt like the van was too small, and I was having trouble breathing. I think I was hallucinating, but it felt like a panic attack. I got out of bed and stepped outside the van to get some fresh air but found that I couldn't stand. Then I felt a shuddering pain in my right side, and I fell to my knees and began convulsing uncontrollably. Something was very, very wrong.

Eventually, the pain and the convulsions passed. I knew I needed to get to an emergency room immediately. But in my weakened state, all I could do was say, "Matt. Matt. Matt. Matt." I kept repeating his name until he woke up and took me to the hospital.

Cut to: an ER doctor telling me I was acting like a fucking ninny. Talk about bedside manner.

I was so confused. There I was, lying in the hospital bed, in unbelievable pain. I could barely talk. I could barely stand. Something was very wrong, and this doctor — whose job was to take care of me — was cursing at me and telling me to leave.

"It's been a fucking guessing game trying to get any information out of you," the doctor said. "It's time for you to leave."

This statement further confused me because I had just told the nurse all my symptoms, which the doctor literally read back to me word for word from the clipboard containing her notes. The doctor left the room, and I asked Matt what the hell was going on. He was just as confused as me, so he followed the doctor into the other room to ask. The doctor told him that I was taking advantage of my best friend, and it was time for him to take me home.

I try to take responsibility for everything in my life, but I have no idea what I did to this doctor to deserve this treatment. Later, I called the hospital to file a formal complaint. I told them not to send me a bill because I wouldn't pay it. But I guess it doesn't work that way. No matter what kind of service they give, whether they help you or not, you still pay. Doesn't sound like a business to me.

Just so you know, if you ever want a doctor to curse at you while you're in pain, it's an experience that costs about $1,500 at Moab Regional Hospital, so start saving your money now.

To this day, I still don't know exactly what happened, but my theory is that the massive amount of bacteria in my gut from the nutritional yeast in the pasta made my body freak out, and the convulsions and hallucinations I experienced were from extreme indigestion. If you've ever had too many probiotics, you know what I mean.

The next morning, I gave myself an enema to flush out my intestines and went back to sleep. A few hours later, I woke again with a strong urge to go to the bathroom and had full-blown diarrhea. I was still having trouble walking, but I made it back from the campground bathroom to the van safely. Unfortunately, I was still getting used to the ins and outs of living in a vehicle, so there were some systems and habits I hadn't yet assimilated. When I reached for the handle, I realized that I had locked myself out. Wonderful.

With no phone or wallet, I went to the campground office to look for somebody who could pick my lock. It turned out the park's handyman had the skills.

"Where'd you learn that?" I asked him.

"Prison," he said.

Very comforting.

You might say I was still learning how to drive. In other words, I was having a hell of a time learning how to adapt to my new lifestyle. But it didn't stop there.

* * *

After we were done camping for Jeep Week, my buddy Matt and his girlfriend went to another event for Passover, and I was left to fend for myself in Moab for a couple of days, where I kept having panic attacks. I slowly came to realize that these attacks were due to a lack of oxygen — altitude sickness, basically.

Once I had the answer, I found a can of oxygen and stopped smoking and drinking, which helped. For so long, I had been at sea level in high humidity, with the creature comforts of a nice cozy apartment. Now I was at a high elevation in a very dry climate with no amenities, and all those creature comforts were looking pretty appealing. I would have killed to have my own Airbnb to just veg out and watch Netflix, but if I was going to be doing this van thing for the next year, I needed to figure out how to adapt.

Where do I sleep? How do I protect myself? How do I start my day? Where do I shower? Those first few nights alone, I had to create a new lifestyle from scratch, in an environment that my body was not liking. Each night, I fell asleep with my heart beating so hard it felt like it was going to leave my chest. My body was in full-fledged fight-or-flight mode. I focused on taking slow, deep breaths and somehow found a way to fall asleep. Once asleep, I actually slept very well and always woke up refreshed, but it was an ongoing struggle.

The truth is, I simply hadn't been prepared for the drastic transition from a very specific daily routine in a high-end apartment to being homeless, with no routine at all, in a new place that my body wasn't used to. I needed to adapt.

Since the altitude was affecting me so drastically, I decided to drive up to Arches National Park — an even higher altitude — to do my morning routine and exercise. Then I descended back down to Moab for the day to do my video editing work at a coffee shop, explore, and relax. That worked well.

Developing a new routine again helped immensely. After that first weekend of living in the van, I felt like a champion. I'd done it! I'd been forced to figure everything out on my own, but doing things the hard way would end up benefitting me in the long run.

It had been tough, but I'd survived my initiation into the vanlife! And after that first hump, everything was painless and beautiful.

Your body and mind are incredible learning machines. They'll find a way to adapt.

When you think about it, the human story is almost unbelievable. We've been through ice ages and saber-toothed tigers, we've lived in caves, we've hunted woolly mammoths, we've figured out how to farm — the genetic history that you are programmed with is pretty incredible. Trust in its ability. Trust in your ability. You can learn to do anything.

Chapter 9:

OFF-ROADING = GETTING OUT OF YOUR COMFORT ZONE

Rocky Mountains, CO — March 2018

I pulled over to a river off the side of the freeway. And against my better judgment, I stripped off my clothes and jumped in.

There was still snow on the ground, but it was the only running water I had seen in a couple of weeks. I needed a shower pretty badly. I was a dirty boy!

Sure did wake me up. COLD!

Partway through washing my crotch with freezing-cold water, I paused to appreciate the fact that just a few short weeks ago, I'd been showering in a fancy tiled bathroom with running hot water and a big mirror so I could groom myself like a domesticated animal. I'd never considered how valuable such inventions were. I'd been so lucky!

What a reversal. I'd gone from a clean-shaven, financially independent, sexy-sports-car-driving business owner to a dirty mountain man living in a van down by the river. And my transformation was complete.

But seriously... you ever pooped in the wild? It's so much more satisfying.

* * *

Not only did discomfort become the norm for me, but I soon developed a taste for it. I was learning how to be comfortable being uncomfortable.

For so long, I had relied on a vast lineup of creature comforts that weren't necessary to my survival. In fact, as I dove deeper and deeper into my new life, I found that most of those comforts had kept me complacent, weak, and sick. I'd been unknowingly limiting myself.

It turned out I didn't need an apartment, bills, the internet, a fridge, running water, heat, or A/C to thrive. Although these things do make life easier, the easy road usually doesn't lead to growth. Sometimes you have to take the more difficult roads to get the results you want.

Nothing worth having comes easy. Get out of your comfort zone. That's where growth happens. And the road of growth always leads to more than you could have possibly imagined.

Chapter 10:

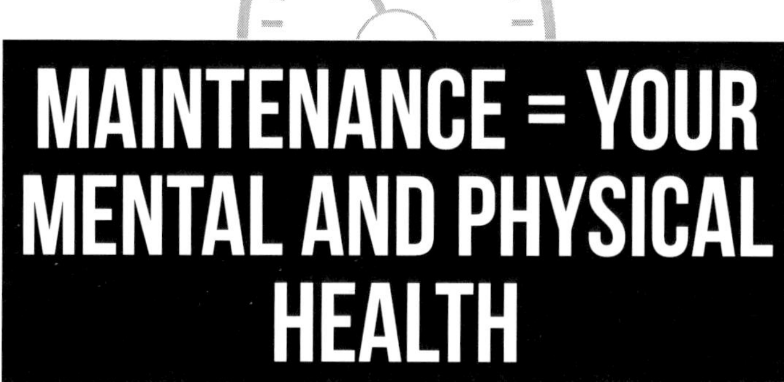

MAINTENANCE = YOUR MENTAL AND PHYSICAL HEALTH

Fort Stockton, TX — April 2018

I woke up and stepped outside to see the whole parking lot bathed in pink light. The sun was just about to crest the Walmart sign.

I headed to the nearest nature spot to start my morning routine underneath the sunrise. I finally felt in harmony with Janüs the van. (I suppose after experiencing hell, everything looks a little brighter.)

After Moab, I had been planning to return to Austin, the starting point of this crazy journey, to make some final adjustments to the van. Instead, I'd decided to take my time and head to Denver. And because I had already overcome the challenges of adaptation, I handled the altitude well and had a wonderful time visiting friends and experiencing the Rockies. I then slowly made my way across Texas, spending the night in a different small town every day. By now, I was finally experiencing the romantic ideal of freedom — you know, the kind you see on Instagram.

Vanlife became effortless because I stayed consistent with my routine: I woke up to watch the sunrise, meditated in nature with a cup of hot water and lemon, journaled, read, exercised, made a protein shake, worked for a few hours at a local coffee shop, ate an American breakfast around noon, drove for a few hours to the next small town, and landed at a movie theater to relax and wind down before parking for the night. Then, the next day, I did it all over again.

This routine was the only way I was able to stay grounded in the midst of so much travel. I found that when I didn't have a plan, I began to panic as flashbacks of Moab returned to haunt me.

When you're in a different place every day with no home base, your routine *becomes* your home. It doesn't matter where you are; if you have the same routine, you'll be fine.

Every once in a while, your vehicle needs a checkup. Oil change, air filter, brake fluid, tire pressure, windshield washer fluid, etc., just like a routine physical or an appointment at the dentist to make sure you're healthy.

Sticking to your vehicle's maintenance schedule can help prevent problems before the dreaded check engine light comes on. But what happens if it comes on, and you choose to ignore it? You'll pay for it later.

The same is true in life. Ignore your check engine light, and you get sick and break down. If the problem isn't fixed, it strains other parts of you, and other things start going wrong because they have to compensate for the original problem.

Unresolved problems beget more problems. Having routines in place can ensure that you stay happy and healthy, especially on the road.

CHAPTER 11:

THROW THE MAP OUT THE WINDOW

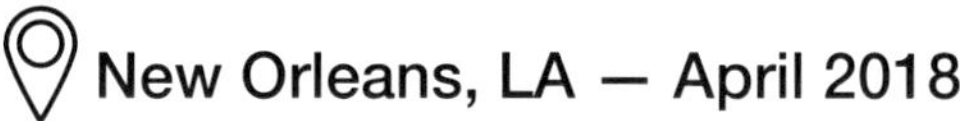

New Orleans, LA — April 2018

> A good traveler has no fixed plans and is not intent on arriving.
>
> —*Lao Tzu*

"Come to my brother's prom with us. He's graduating this year. Dress nice."

That was the extent of the text sent to me by my buddy Julian.

Okay, sure.

Next thing I know, I'm at the high school just outside New Orleans, arriving just in time. I wanted to look sharp, so I busted out my money suit that my mom made me — literally a suit tailored with one-hundred-dollar bills printed on the fabric. Louisiana was hot, and changing in the van was enough for me to have worked up a sweat already.

Inside the cool air conditioning of the high school, a couple of students kindly introduced themselves to me. My money suit was a hit. But these students weren't like any high school students I had ever met. I finally found Julian and his family taking their prom pictures with his brother Gabe and Gabe's girlfriend. (Gabe had Down syndrome, which I'd already been aware of. His girlfriend looked a little different as well.)

"What do you like about Gabe?" I asked her.

She shrugged her shoulders. "He's handsome," is all she said. Then Gabe posed for her, and she groped his muscles. Adorable.

I then noticed an African American student following Julian around. She also appeared to have Down syndrome, but that didn't stop her from shaking her booty and showing off for Julian. She wouldn't leave him alone. "She did this last year, too," Julian remarked. Apparently, she had even gotten down on one knee and asked Julian to marry her.

Slowly, the situation became clear. This was a prom for students with special needs. Julian had failed to make that clear to me, not that it mattered. The only thing about the situation that bothered me a little was that I didn't like the idea of kids with special needs being separated from the "normal" kids.

I could have very easily felt uncomfortable about this unexpected situation and just left. But by that point in my van adventure, discomfort had become the norm anyway, so the only thing left to do was have fun and make a memory of it. So it was time to dance. We danced our butts off with the students and had a great time.

My biggest takeaway was that I was surprised at how social and outgoing these students were. At one point, another African American student (the population in this part of Louisiana is 80–90% African American) took a liking to me, calling me "money man." He was fascinated by my suit and kept touching me, which would normally have made me a little uncomfortable, but I knew it was harmless. He was also impressed that I was a filmmaker — he had an interest in film as well and wanted to be an actor. Later, his buddy came over, who was a little shy, and I introduced myself. I talked to them for a while about their passions, their dreams, what they enjoyed doing most. I encouraged them to pursue those good feelings.

Bottom line: Have fun. What other reason is there to live?

***

Louisiana was a blast. Not just because of the festivals and drunken partying in the French Quarter, but because of the culture! The food, the vibe, the people, the Southern hospitality, the giving, the love, the history… I've never experienced such rich culture anywhere else in the United States.

Julian and his family took me in with open arms and showed me the best time. They wined and dined me at their restaurant, Don's Seafood, which is famous for bringing Cajun seafood to the masses. Then they invited me to stay with them at their fishing camp in the bayou for the following weekend. I was only planning on staying in Louisiana for one weekend, but I couldn't pass up an opportunity like this. So I decided to say yes and stay an extra week to take them up on their offer. As important as planning is, sometimes you just gotta throw the map and the itinerary out the window and wing it.

Since I'd begun living in the van, I had committed to being more spontaneous. And this decision to live an actively spontaneous life was a great exercise in improvisation. I had some friends in college who performed in Comedy Sportz, a competitive youth improv league, and I had learned from them that the only rule of improv is: "Yes, and!" Meaning, if you get a suggestion, you have to accept ("yes") and then expand on it ("and").

Driving to the fishing camp was surreal. There was hardly any ground to stand on beyond the dirt road. It was all water and wetlands, with black weeping willows growing up out of the smelly marshes on either side of the road. The air was thick with biting flies and a strange musk. I felt like I was in prehistoric times.

When I got to the camp, the air smelled like sulfur. All the houses were on stilts, and each had its own dock and boat in the channel that led out to the "boot" of Louisiana and then to the ocean. For the seafaring locals, these channels are like a system of freeways.

The sun set over the water shortly after I arrived, and I sat on the dock with Gabe and his mother Julia, watching the beautiful pink, orange, and red sky. We talked about family, parenting, and the challenges and gifts of being a mother to a child with special needs while Gabe strutted around flexing his muscles and catching crabs. We talked until the bugs became intolerable. The conversation was intimate and endearing. I felt so welcome there, like I was part of the family. It was a family experience I had never had before.

But the highlight of the trip was, of course, the fishing. (They don't call it a fishing camp for nothing.)

Nobody else wanted to get up at 4 a.m., so it was just me and Julian's Dad. We got some shrimp for bait from a neighbor who had his own shrimping boat and set out in the dark of early morning. The sun was just barely coming up when we got to the first spot. But the waters were too rough to fish there, so we moved on to another spot outside the main channel, where it was far less windy.

The bayou is fascinating. We wove our way through an archipelago of tiny islands of marshland surrounded by seemingly endless stretches of water. I hadn't caught a fish since I was a kid, but fishing in the bayou is like shooting a bowl of goldfish with a shotgun. I had forgotten how fun it was.

We caught *a lot* of fish that day. But they're smart — I lost just as many pieces of bait as fish I caught. We put them on ice to save them for dinner that night, watched the sunrise from the boat, drank some morning beers, and had some laughs. On our way back home, the water wasn't rough anymore. It was beautiful and glassy. We were flying at 60 mph all the way home. And I took a nice nap when we got back.

That night, we gutted and cleaned our catch. I had never gutted a fish before, but the process is exactly what it sounds like. Then we cooked all of our seafood Cajun-style! That means deep-fried in batter with special secret sauce (to be honest, I think it was ketchup and mayonnaise). It was so freaking delicious.

We lived off the land that entire weekend. The only food we bought was beer, eggs, chips. What a world.

* * *

The morning before we left, I had brunch with some gators at an old church converted into a restaurant. No joke, they had a pond with some very large alligators that you could walk right up to. The colorful mosaic church windows cast a rainbow glow over me as I ate my tasty Southern breakfast.

When we got back from the fishing camp, Julia invited me to stay with them at their house in LaPlace. I was honored. I spent that Sunday poolside, drinking with the kids and playing water basketball with Gabe. I wrote Julia a nice thank-you card, thanking her for the Southern hospitality and for opening her arms to me, including me in the family, and giving me a family experience I had never known. I spent the rest of the day on the golf course with Julian. Not golfing, really. Just driving around in their pimped-out, chrome-wheeled golf cart and causing trouble — drinking, smoking, and chasing alligators.

You might ask, was this the most efficient use of my time? My answer: Who cares? After all, the point of vanlife was FREEDOM — having the freedom to do what I wanted, when I wanted, with whomever I wanted. And if I hadn't made the choice to spontaneously alter my schedule in pursuit of a little fun, I would have missed this amazing time.

The real question is, how much are *you* missing?

There is value in planning everything to a T, to be sure. But sometimes, you just gotta throw the roadmap out the window and wing it.

My experience at the fishing camp was one of the highlights of the year. And it was all because I said, "YES, AND..." When you're invited to be part of a cool experience, when somebody suggests you go someplace, or when an opportunity presents itself, do it! You'll find yourself part of some pretty amazing experiences. This is how you live life to the fullest.

It is fatal to know too much at the outset: boredom comes too quickly to the traveler who knows his own route as to the novelist how is over certain of his plot.

Paul Theroux, To the Ends of the Earth

CHAPTER 12:

FLYING SOLO

Santa Fe, TX — April 2018

On my way back from an awesome time in Louisiana, I was experiencing withdrawal after all the fun and was feeling a little lonely. Life on the road isn't all puppies and rainbows. It can be very challenging to be so independent.

It was around this time that I noticed that all the American flags were at half-mast. I wondered why, so I looked it up and learned that there had been a school shooting earlier that very day in Southeast Texas, not far from where I was.

School shootings really bother me. So much so that I began writing a script about a school shooting while on the road, inspired by a true story of a high school football coach in Portland who disarmed a school shooter with a hug. And since I was in unfamiliar storytelling territory and needed a better understanding of the subject matter, I decided to check it out.

I headed to Santa Fe High School, but by the time I got there, there wasn't much to see. Everything was blocked off and overrun with police and reporters. I talked to a few people to see if I could get some insider information. Ten killed, ten others wounded. The only other detail I heard was that it had started in the art room. That hit close to home for me.

Why would I choose to write about such a dark and challenging subject? Because it bothered me, and I wanted to do something about it. But it's still so hard to write about.

Why? That's the only word that comes to mind. Why would this happen?

When I study these school shooters and the atrocities they've committed, I have to consciously protect myself. I imagine a bubble forming around me that acts as a shield from all the pain and hatred and evil. It's the only way I can dive into such subject matter. Why would anybody ever do something like this? And why does it happen so frequently? I believe it has something to do with the fact that we are living out of alignment with who we truly are, like Austin's box bomber. Our environment and lifestyle have grown far beyond what our biology has been doing for hundreds of thousands of years. Some might even consider our way of life to be unnatural — inhuman.

My theory is that our biology can't evolve quickly enough to keep up with the rapid changes in our environment. As a result, I think some of us end up feeling lost and disconnected, which we're told means we need to be medicated with pharmaceutical drugs that do more harm than good. In reality, all we probably need is a good organic meal, some exercise, sunshine, and, most of all, a friend to talk to.

It makes me so sad. I can't let it continue. But I don't know what to do about it other than what I'm best at: making movies.

* * *

Visiting Santa Fe High School just hours after this incident was another wake-up call. Why do these incidents affect me so much? Because I've been there before.

I feel like I know these shooters. I've struggled with mental illness before, and I'm very familiar with how it can warp one's perspective of reality. It's a strange sickness, to say the least. Most of the time, I didn't even know I was sick. And the worst part was that it made me want to be alone, when that was the *opposite* of what I needed for my mental health.

It was a beautiful day, so after leaving Santa Fe High School, I went to Galveston to swim in the gulf for a bit. As I sat on the beach in the warm sun by myself, I felt an instinct to turn to somebody and share the ecstasy of the moment. But there was nobody there. And suddenly, I feared that I might be slipping into my own solitary confinement.

Being self-employed, I already struggled with being alone. Even when I had my fancy apartment in Austin, I had no community to tap into other than a couple of friends. With the van, I feared I was further isolating myself. Now, there were even fewer people whom I could relate to. I mean, honestly, how many people live in their vehicles? I felt even more different and disconnected than before.

I couldn't help but wonder, had I made a mistake? Was the vanlife really a good idea for me?

Flying solo is no easy task. I recommend a copilot. Admittedly, this comes with its own set of challenges. But we humans aren't meant to do life alone.

There's a reason solitary confinement is used as a punishment in prison. Get connected on this journey called life.

Chapter 13:

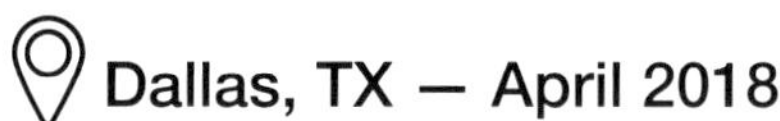

I sat beside my buddy Mike, still shocked at what had just happened. But at least my seat was comfortable — we were lounging in a set of display furniture inside a Walmart. We were also soaking wet, on a high from having just escaped a flash flood.

Why Walmart? Well, we'd been looking for a place to relax and process what had just happened, and we hadn't known where else to go. The Walmart, for some reason, seemed like the most appropriate place.

Finally, we decided to go find a bar instead. We needed a drink! The only problem: When we got back to Mike's car, something wasn't right... The entire front bumper was missing. How had we not noticed that? I have no idea.

So, a little backstory. I had left the van in Austin temporarily to fly to Phoenix, Los Angeles, and Dallas to shoot a series of interviews for a client, which had gone well. Afterward, I hitched a ride from my buddy Mike to head back to the airport, but there were some foreboding clouds on the horizon.

On the road, traffic was backed up due to some high water. Several times, we were met with washes where entire sections of the road were covered with water. But we were already running late because of the weather, so Mike floored it, fording straight through each time. Until we reached a particular puddle.

This time, we didn't float through to the other side. Instead, we slammed into a wall of water... and sank.

The engine went dead almost immediately, flooded. Apparently, this puddle was concealing a wash used specifically for channeling flash floods, making it deeper than it appeared.

We were officially stuck in a flash flood!

The water was up to the sides of the doors and getting higher. My film equipment was in the back of the car — maybe $30,000 worth of gear. So I had a choice. I could sit and wait for the car to flood, or I could get out and do something about it.

I didn't even think about it. I acted immediately.

I recall taking off my shoes and socks, then emptying my pockets. After that, I don't really remember much. The next thing I knew, I was on top of Mike's car, screaming at the top of my lungs.

Mike later retold the full story: Apparently, I first tried to open the door, but the water was too high. And when rolling down the window didn't work either, I crawled out of the sunroof and jumped into the dirty water flowing through the street, which was by now up to my waist. I waded through the river, around to the back of the car, and tried to push it up the hill and out of the water. It didn't move an inch.

"Put it in neutral! Put it in neutral!" I screamed like an animal.

Mike put it in neutral. Like I said, this whole experience passed in a blur for me, but according to Mike, when I pushed again, the car moved.

I don't know where this superhuman strength came from, but I was pumping pure adrenaline. I physically pushed the car up the street until it was out of the water and my equipment was safe from the flood. The floor of the vehicle was already soaked. Close call.

Mike says I then went around to the front of the vehicle to get back in the car, but when I opened the door, I instead jumped up onto the hood of the car and screamed, "That's how we fuckin' do it! That's how we fuckin' do it!" I beat the hood of the car, adrenaline and testosterone pumping through my veins. That was when I came to. It all happened so fast. I felt like an animal!

I do have one brief flash of a memory amid the chaos of that moment: the image of a bumper floating down the river. I just didn't put two and two together until later, in the Walmart parking lot, when we noticed that Mike's poor car was missing a piece.

After the Walmart, we made our way to Twin Peaks, drank *a lot* of beer, and got a waitress's number. Worth it.

We never made it to the airport, so I missed my next interview. I guess I just wasn't supposed to get on that plane.

What do you do when you run into obstacles?

Potholes, dead ends, breaking down, construction zones, flat tires, getting lost, closed roads, wrong turns, rerouting, wrong way… We like to believe that we live in a material world that is predictable and controllable. But in reality, roadblocks happen on a daily basis. Almost nothing goes exactly as expected. That's LIFE!

So how do you handle these obstacles? My advice: Don't try to avoid them. Instead, embrace them. Take them head-on. Because that's how you learn and grow.

CHAPTER 14:

FACE YOUR FEARS

Tucson, AZ — May 2018

I woke up early and felt like going on a nice long run for some reason. So I made my way to the nearest available slice of nature, near the base of the mountains in Sabino Canyon, where I found a series of trails looping around for over ten miles. Several signs warned of the danger of mountain lions.

I hoped to run the five miles to Seven Falls (I just liked the name), then run back. That would be ten miles total, which I was hoping to do in an hour and a half. But you know how it goes — almost never as expected.

The terrain was not conducive to running. It was very rocky, difficult to even hike. This was mostly bouldering territory. It took much longer than expected, and when I got to Seven Falls, there were no waterfalls. Just a small pond. Still, it was scenic and kind of nice, so I climbed around to the back of the pond to take a picture of the view with the new GoPro I'd recently purchased for my van adventures. I got it out of my trail backpack and promptly dropped it. I could only watch as it slid down the slick rock and straight into the pond.

Oh, boy…

Did I mention that I have a fear of stagnant bodies of water? Not sure why. I enjoy the water in general. I have no problem with the ocean, pools, jacuzzies, rivers, lakes — I even love cold showers. But if I can't see the bottom, I have trouble with it, especially if I know there are creatures lurking below.

The new GoPro had only cost $250 and would be easy to replace. But the card had some footage on it that I wanted to keep, so I was a little frustrated. The weather was starting to heat up, and I knew it would take me at least an hour to run back to the van. I had to get back soon. I took a deep breath and made peace with the fact that I would never see my GoPro or the footage on it ever again. But for some reason, I couldn't bring myself to leave.

Looking back, I can see that vanlife had instilled within me a new sense of determination. The last thing I wanted was to go for a swim in this strange stagnant body of water, yet I just couldn't let this go. The GoPro was waterproof, so the camera would be fine, but the pond's surface was coated with floating green moss, and bubbles were surfacing every once in a while, which could only mean one thing. Creatures.

I was about five miles from safety. If something happened to me, I was screwed. I couldn't let it go. But I also couldn't stand there mulling it over while temperatures continued to rise, leaving me exposed to the dangerous midday heat. So I had to make a decision: Jump in the water and retrieve my new GoPro, or leave now to get back to the van before it got too hot.

The old me would have given up, but the new me could not justify the tiny fears that were standing in the way of a good story and retrieving my beloved camera. So I set my stuff down and made my way to the edge of the water.

The banks consisted of slippery rocks all the way down to the bottom of the pond, so I had to be mindful. I put one leg into the water. *Cold*. Then another leg. *Colder!* Slowly but surely, I lowered myself into the water until it was up to my chest.

My body began to panic from the cold, and my breathing became quick and erratic. I couldn't see the bottom, and I felt my chest tighten. Fear was taking over. But instead of freaking out, I just took a deep breath. Because of my cold showers, my body knew what to do. So

I just stood there for a minute or so, focusing on my breathing until I calmed down and got used to it.

I began probing the pond floor with my feet and soon found a hard object. I bent down and picked it up: just a rock. I had apparently discovered a great new way to retrieve river rocks, because I proceeded to do the same thing about five more times.

At one point, I noticed bubbles that seemed to be coming toward me. Logic told me that there was very little chance that this pond contained piranha nor anything poisonous... I mean, it's Arizona, not the Congo. But snapping turtles? In reality, there was probably a better chance that I would contract a bacterial infection than get eaten by something. I used this logic to talk myself out of another panic attack. But as the sun shifted in the sky, the pond was being overtaken by shadows cast from the rocks above, and I was getting colder by the minute.

After about half an hour of searching for my sunken camera, I finally gave up and headed out of the pond. As I was reaching for a handhold in a small crevice between two hunks of rock to pull myself up, my hand landed on a flat object that was too smooth to be a rock. I looked down in disbelief at the GoPro in my hand. It hadn't fallen to the bottom of the pond where I'd been foraging. It had only gone a couple of feet and gotten stuck in a crack. Success!

When I finally got out of the water, camera in hand, I noticed a ginormous spider sitting on the rock right beside where I'd gotten into the water. It was as big as the palm of my hand, no exaggeration, and so well camouflaged that I hadn't noticed it before. Its comfortable perch on the edge of a rock jutting out over the pond gave it a great overlook of the water — right by my face while I'd been rummaging around. But, like whatever had produced the bubbles in the pond, I don't think it had any interest in eating me. Just a fun little joke played on me by nature.

I got into the sun and took off my smelly wet clothes. I was about to strip naked to dry off in the sun when I noticed some hikers coming down to the pond, so I settled for my underwear. It was getting hot by that time, and drying off didn't take long. As I left, the hikers asked me to take a picture of them.

"Watch out for water spiders," I said. "You can't see them because they're camouflaged."

Victory! I ran all the way back from that pond — only to discover a parking ticket waiting for me on my windshield. Doh!

I went into the park office and told them what had happened. Fortunately, they were nice enough to wave the fine. (They probably just wanted me to leave because I smelled so bad. I was in desperate need of a shower.)

I found the closest YMCA, which is always free on your first visit. Their facilities featured a large, open shower where you have the unique privilege of showering with a bunch of old, saggy, naked men. But I didn't care. I hadn't showered in days. Why do old guys like YMCA so much?

* * *

In my daily meditation practice, I have the unique opportunity to observe my mind, and it's interesting to see what the mind does. Its job is to survive, so it's wired to worry about everything.

We evolved during a time when conditions were mostly inhospitable. If the sub-freezing temperatures didn't kill you, the lack of food would. That or a saber-toothed tiger. But the thing is, we no longer live in that environment. There are no more saber-toothed tigers, and for most of us, droughts, food shortages, and hostile enemies are no longer everyday occurrences.

We now live in a magical world where everything is done for us! Our biology, however, hasn't evolved much since the ice age, which means our brains are still wired the same way. So what does your clever brain do to compensate? It finds new threats that really aren't very threatening at all.

I've noticed that the vast majority of my fearful thoughts never actually manifest. The National Science Foundation estimates that the average human has 12,000–60,000 thoughts per day, 80% of which are negative, and 95% of which are the same repetitive thoughts from the previous day. According to Dr. Robert Leahy, PhD, 85% of what you worry about actually never happens. And of the remaining 15%

that do happen, 79% of those happenings actually end up being positive learning experiences or easier to handle than expected.

Translation: 97% of what you worry about amounts to nothing but unnecessary mind games.

Face your fears.

You *will* win because there's nothing to fear but fear itself.

Chapter 15:

COMMUNE WITH NATURE

Page, AZ — May 2018

It was the busiest Walmart I'd ever seen. The parking lot was filled with all kinds of RVs and vans with license plates from all over the country.

Apparently, Page, Arizona is a major intersection for many cross-country and long-distance road-trippers from all directions, which makes it a common stop for vehicle-dwellers like me. I found the restaurants to be just as busy, as it took me twenty minutes to get a table for one at the local Mexican place, another twenty minutes to order, and another twenty to get my food. But they had hundreds of different kinds of tequilas to help pass the time. (I tried the one with Frida Kahlo on the bottle.)

I was on my way to Sedona, Arizona for a film festival that was premiering a film I had just finished, so I researched cool things to do in Arizona. Little-known fact: Arizona is one of the most interesting states in the country because it contains five different climate zones, including mountains and snow! It's not *all* hot and dry!

Because of the vast range of elevations in Arizona, it has a wide variety of temperatures and, therefore, precipitation swings. This produces crazy thunderstorms and flash floods, which form some interesting natural land formations. One of the most popular images on travel blogs and Instagram Stories from this area is a beautifully ethereal, curvy red canyon carved out by water. For some reason, this curvy red canyon always stuck with me. It looked so magical, and I had always wanted to go there. Lo and behold, Antelope Canyon was located in Page, Arizona. And since I was headed to Sedona, I decided to take a few days to explore the natural beauty of northern Arizona.

That morning, I watched the sunrise from a red hill overlooking the sea of mobile homes parked at Walmart. I decided to head to Antelope Canyon a little early because I'd heard that the best time to witness it was when the light changes in the morning.

I arrived at 8 a.m., but it was already packed with people. What I learned at the ticket booth was that the canyon is on Native American reservation land, so you can't just hike through it. You need to be accompanied by a Native American guide. And since it is one of the most popular tourist destinations in Arizona, the guides lead tours of a dozen or so visitors at a time, which also means you can't experience it on your own. The cost: $50.

Do I really want to spend $50 to have a guy lead me through a canyon with a bunch of tourists I don't know? I thought. *Pass.*

I left the booth. But as tours began leaving on their journeys, I reconsidered.

This is probably one of those once-in-a-lifetime experiences. I should do it now while I have the chance, or else I'll regret it. So I went back.

The line for the tours was probably a hundred people deep, but somehow, I found my way into a tour that was leaving immediately and needed just one more person to reach capacity. My tour was full of visitors from Denmark, motorcycling from Canada to Mexico. They were very friendly, but we were constantly standing in the way of each other's pictures.

As we descended into the canyon on foot, the temperature dropped. Stairs built into the canyon walls led us downward, zig-zagging into darker and darker crevices until we reached a soft, sandy bottom. As my eyes slowly adjusted, our guide explained the rules. No cameras.

Just phones. Follow the leader. Don't touch anything. And he led us through a dark maze, crisscrossing through the carved earth.

Everything looked blue in the darkness, to the point that I was beginning to wonder if we would see anything interesting at all. But gradually, our surroundings got brighter and brighter. Then he took us around a corner that opened up into a large shaft, and my jaw dropped.

A solitary shaft of sunlight at the tippy top of the canyon bounced off of the sandy walls, creating a cascade of brilliant light all the way down to the bottom where we stood. There were so many colors on the canyon walls, from orange to red to purple to blue. It was the most breathtaking thing I've ever seen. Like God dipped his paintbrush in a rainbow. No wonder I'd seen so many amazing images of this place — it was impossible to take a bad picture. Everywhere you looked was picturesque. Worth every penny. And to think I had almost passed it up! This was exactly what Janüs the van was made for.

After we climbed back out of the canyon, I felt like a new person. What had I just experienced? The canyon's magnificence was magnified when I stopped to consider that this aesthetic harmony had been created by nothing but sandstone, water, and sunlight.

Antelope Canyon became my new safe space. To this day, whenever I need a safe place to retreat and recharge, I meditate, imagining I am walking through the cascading rainbow of Antelope Canyon.

Three pieces of paper is what I gave in exchange for this unforgettable experience. Two twenties and a ten.

The rest of that day, I explored Horseshoe Bend and the North Rim of the Grand Canyon. More rock carved by water! I arrived in Sedona that night and had a delicious meal at a fancy restaurant. (Believe it or not, I ate rattlesnake.)

Go outside more often!

Nature is incredibly healing. For hundreds of thousands of years, we've been living outside, at one with nature — in the sun all day long, growing and eating plants, bathing in rivers and oceans, traveling with the seasons. Only in the

> **past few hundred years have we separated ourselves from our source of life. Nature is where we came from, and it is to nature that we will inevitably return.**

For me, living in a van unlocked my ancient genetics by forcing me to live at one with nature, be outside more, wake with the sun, and travel with the seasons. When you choose to experience the country from the road, you'll find that most of your time is spent outside of cities, on long strips of highways that are surrounded by hundreds of miles of nature. It will take you less than an hour to drive through a city (depending on the traffic), but you can drive for many hours between cities, seeing nothing but farms and natural wilderness.

We live in an incredibly abundant country. And from the road, urban centers soon began to feel strange, depressing, and unnatural to me. I found myself wanting to spend more and more time avoiding major metropolises in order to commune more with nature.

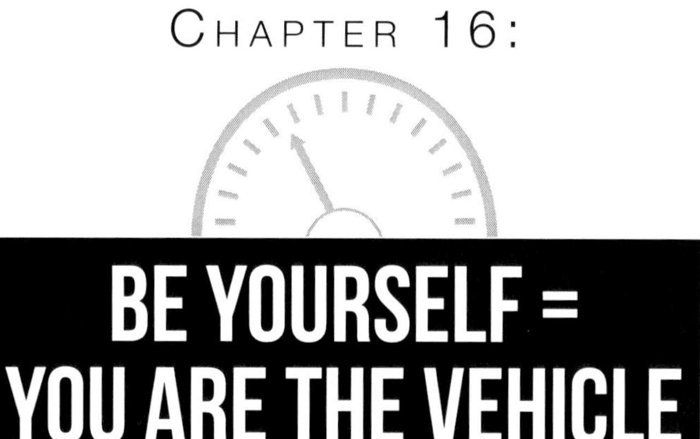

Chapter 16: Be Yourself = You Are the Vehicle

Sedona, AZ — June 2018

I walked onstage as hundreds of people cheered. They had just finished watching a documentary film that I had been working on for the previous four years. It's interesting how just a few seconds of recognition can wash away the road rash from four years of grind and hustle.

The Illuminate Film Festival was an overwhelmingly positive experience for me, beyond what I ever could have imagined. Being around a swarm of other conscious filmmakers who wanted to help the world just like me was, just as the name implied, illuminating. Not to mention that the magical energy of Sedona created a vortex in which anything seemed possible. Instant karma was in the air. Anything I desired or envisioned happened almost instantly.

To prepare for the event, I'd hired a personal coach for the first time. I felt like I needed help to ensure that I'd be at my best to get the most out of my experience there. It was money well spent because she helped me get crystal clear about my intentions for the film festival and to define who I wanted to be while I was there.

One of the best things she did for me was to make me completely comfortable with who I was. One of my intentions for the festival was to make real and lasting connections with people in the biz who could actually help me get to where I wanted to go in my career. This would require that I talk to people I didn't know. The problem was… I have never been very outgoing. In fact, I was pretty quiet and introverted.

Isn't that interesting? I had always struggled with loneliness, but I'd never felt comfortable talking to new people. Sounds like a self-fulfilling prophecy to me. Maybe the problem stemmed from trust issues. Maybe it was a matter of self-worth. Or maybe I just didn't like people. I don't know! But all that started to change while I was living in the van.

I quickly found a real need to connect to people while on the road. This primed me to make a real, substantial change, and my coach helped me secure a new mindset with daily affirmations:

- I love myself. I am worthy. I am enough.
- I am not afraid to be myself in public and share myself with the world because I'm FUCKING AWESOME.
- I am unabashedly, unashamedly, un-embarrassingly 110% NICK-fucking-CONEDERA!
- I express my feelings without shame or guilt or fear.
- I accept myself FIRST.
- I allow myself to be ME — without shame or guilt or fear.

What do you think would happen if you screamed affirmations like these at the top of your lungs every day? Try it out and see how you feel (preferably if you have some privacy)! That's what I did every morning in my hotel suite until I truly believed what I was saying. And the strangest thing happened… It worked.

I became me.

* * *

While in Sedona, I heard about a cool three-day screenwriting workshop that was being put on immediately after the festival. But there was no way to get in. I would have had to apply months prior, and submissions had already closed.

I was a little upset about this because if I had heard about it before, I would have applied right away. Documentary work was an easy way to pay the bills, but I wanted to be a screenwriter and director! I wracked my brain trying to think of ways to crash the workshop. But that instant karma was in the air, so I asked the festival organizers how to get in. I kept hearing the same thing: “It’s full.” Until I talked to the right person, and the answer changed to, “Actually, somebody just got sick and dropped out, so there may be an opening. Email me your submission script.”

Later that night, I was having a good time at the festival-sponsored Filmmakers Meet-and-Greet taking place at a local bar/restaurant with delicious food. Everybody kept giving me drink tickets, which was ironic since I had decided not to drink while at the festival. In the middle of it all, the executive director of the festival, surrounded by an entourage, walked straight up to me.

“You’re in the screenwriting workshop,” she said without hesitation.

I didn’t know exactly how to respond.

“We normally wouldn’t do this for just anybody,” she went on, “but we’re doing it for you because you’re you.”

At that moment, I was so overwhelmed with love and gratitude that I started crying right in front of her. My intention to be comfortable being me had paid off tenfold. Because I had committed to being wholly *me*, my energy had begun to resonate at a higher frequency, and others were picking up on it.

I became a master networker and met the coolest filmmakers, all of whom I highly respect. But, more importantly, I created some deep connections with dear friends whom I still care about very much. It was strange at first because I was a different me than I had ever been before. I had completely transformed.

Once I saw that nothing bad was going to happen when I got out of my shell, something shifted within me. And that new me never really went away.

* * *

The screenwriters' workshop took place at a fancy resort where all meals were provided by a fantastic local organic vegan caterer. Here, we focused on the process of taking our film ideas from script to screen. And on the final day of the workshop, to solidify the work that we had just done, the facilitators led us through a guided meditation.

I found myself in the middle of a luscious jungle. Birds chirping, insects buzzing. Everything was vibrant and *alive*!

The palm fronds parted to reveal a crystal temple. It was shining white but a little translucent and smooth like glass. Massive but minimal — just a simple dome shape. As I approached, stairs came out of the temple base, inviting me to a massive door. Above the door was etched the name of the temple: *CONSCIOUSNESS*.

I walked up the stairs, and the door opened all by itself. Inside were twelve massive glass pillars. As I approached each pillar, it lit up from the inside, revealing an epic image of a hero on a journey. Each pillar was a step in the hero's journey depicting the hero being tested in a different way. But this wasn't the archetypal hero's journey; as I got closer, I saw that the images were actually of me on my own journey through life with Janüs the van.

I arrived at the altar, which was empty. I turned back to the door through which I had entered and, to my amazement, saw that the temple was filled with my audience. Who were they? Millions of artists, independents, entrepreneurs, creatives, rebels, and misfits just like me. What did they need? Leadership, guidance, a bright light to show the way — a symbol of hope that they, too, could make their dreams come true, live to their fullest potential, and impact the world in a positive way.

I turned back around to the altar and saw myself. I was lecturing, freely offering my gifts to my audience. And I realized, *It's me that they need. They need to see me enlightened and alive, living to my fullest potential, living my dreams, living my purpose, so they can see what's possible and what they're capable of.*

I finally left the temple. As I walked back down the stairs, the temple behind me slowly crumbled into sand and blew away in the wind. And when I reached the bottom of the stairs, I turned back around to see that it had vanished completely in the sands of time. But a voice whispered from somewhere else, "You can always return to this place."

I opened my eyes and was transported back to the retreat center. Whoa.

This visualization solidified for me the professional and personal gain I experienced at the festival. I wouldn't have received this gift if I hadn't committed to being completely and utterly me.

I am an introvert by nature. I keep to myself, stay behind the camera, and need a lot of privacy and alone time. But because I had been so intentional about my purpose at the festival, I allowed myself to be *me* without shame or guilt or fear. I let myself out of my shell for the first time and shared myself with the world. And the response was overwhelming.

I've been to *a lot* of festivals like this one, but none of them have ever come close to what I experienced at Illuminate 2018. Professionally, I reached a level of influence I hadn't even thought possible, making two dozen contacts in the industry who could help change the trajectory of my career, as well as many others I knew I could help with my skills and contacts (and I did). These included people at Netflix, Gaia, various streaming platforms, theater distributors, foreign distributors, funders, Hollywood producers, Oscar-nominated filmmakers, and consultants to the stars, all of whom had the same values and mission as me: to elevate consciousness.

Something had shifted in me. I was changed.

Had I reached my destination? This elusive place known as "freedom"?

On the road of life, you are the vehicle. So what kind of vehicle are you? A big rig that hauls goods to people in need? A stylish sports car that turns heads and burns rubber? Maybe a four-wheel-drive Jeep that can survive in the wild, drive through rivers, and climb mountains? Or a practical, reliable, economical, long-lasting hybrid with good gas mileage? Or perhaps you're a sports utility vehicle — the Swiss army knife of automobiles.

In order to be fully and utterly you, you must know your vehicle. You must know yourself. Who are you, deep down?

Please don't be afraid to be you. You're fucking awesome, and you don't need anybody else's permission to be you. You are loved. You are worthy.

> Know Thyself.
>
> —*Ancient Greek maxim*

Chapter 17: TALK TO STRANGERS

Jerome, AZ — June 2018

As I watched a T-rex dance on stage with a cowboy singer, it occurred to me that perhaps I had drunk too much.

What brought me to this strange little bar in this tiny town? The magic of Sedona was still in me.

After the Illuminate Film Festival, I was hired to work on a couple of projects that kept me in Sedona for a while. I met a nice older couple at the festival who let me crash with them for a few days. (Turned out, they were nudists.)

Coming down from the high of a consciousness-expanding experience in a magical place around a bunch of conscious artists trying to change the world just like me, my heart was more open than it had ever been before. It's interesting what happens when you're willing to share yourself with perfect strangers. They open themselves to you as well, and through these open avenues, you find yourself being attracted like a magnet to other resonant frequencies. The more palpable the frequency, the stronger the magnet. And you can find yourself being pulled toward interesting destinations.

After the festival, I explored Sedona a bit. I hiked some vortexes. I jumped off a cliff into a river. I ate rattlesnake, buffalo, and elk at a cowboy restaurant. I shopped for crystals. I hung out with superconscious healers. You know, all the usual Sedona stuff.

My mom kept telling me about a restaurant in Jerome called The Asylum — a former mental hospital that had been turned into a hotel and restaurant. I had to check it out. The food was delicious, and I think they thought I was some famous actor from the festival or something because when I asked for vegetables with my hummus instead of pita, they brought me an entire tray of every type of vegetable you can imagine. After dinner, I wasn't done being social, which was strange. I don't remember ever having the desire to be social. Nevertheless, the hostess directed me to the bar down the street — live music tonight!

I had another drink, danced, and talked to strangers. In the course of a single night, I met a cowboy singer, a dancing T-rex, an American Ninja Warrior, an actual geologist looking for gold, and a pinup model who wanted to take naked pictures of me. All at the same bar in this tiny mining town with fewer than 1,000 people. Whaaaaat the heck was going on? It was like I was stuck in some sort of alternate reality. But this is what happens when you put yourself out there.

* * *

My surreal night out in Jerome barely scratches the surface of all the interesting people I met on the road.

In Utah, I met a climber who holds the world record for the most summits of El Capitan.

In Florida, I met a group of magicians who lived together in a magic castle with a dolphin trainer.

In Arkansas, I met a retired police officer charged with murder six times but never convicted.

In the Bay Area, I met a former CIA agent.

In Ogden, I met a professional fighter dressed in a blanket and a fanny pack who lived in a three-story maze of a gym.

In Washington, a farmer named Bone told me, "I once belched into a mic for fifteen minutes for an open mic."

In Atlanta, I met a Walmart security guard who was secretly a superhero. At night, she became The Evangel! A super evangelist fighting evil with her powers of healing, spreading the gospel, and summoning the power of Christ. No, I'm not kidding.

In San Marcos, I met a mycologist who had collected the most venomous snakes in the world. "Oh, hold on a sec," he said after opening the door. "The black mamba got out." Instead of attack dogs, he had a cobra, a sidewinder, a baby rattler, a water moccasin, and several others.

I know you were always told as a kid, "Don't talk to strangers." But nothing good happens when you're too shy to come out of your shell.

Don't be shy. Talk to strangers.

People are wonderful, and humanity is too gloriously diverse to pass up the experience of expanding your horizons by meeting new people. You never know who you will meet! On the road, your nomad energy tends to coax the most interesting people out of their hiding holes.

Chapter 18:

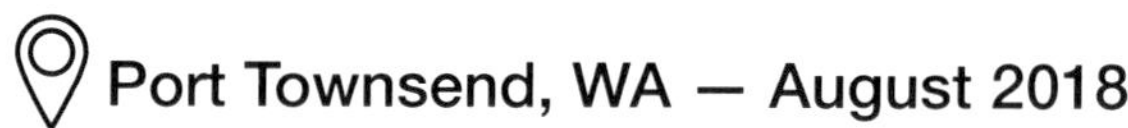

YOU ARE THE DRIVER

Port Townsend, WA — August 2018

My body hurt, and my back ached. That's what happens after eight hours of physical labor. My gears needed some oil.

I was starving, but I still needed to get groceries. So I stepped outside with a pickaxe, dug up some carrots, snagged some fresh kale, snipped a couple of cucumbers, and bagged some USDA Organic Yukon Gold potatoes from the barn. That's life on the farm.

I've always wondered... Where does my food come from? We eat three meals a day, yet most of us have no idea where our food comes from. Costa Rica? Down the street? I had no idea. And I wanted to change that.

Every day, we eat food that has traveled hundreds, maybe even thousands of miles to reach our plates. The next time you sit down to eat, before you devour your plate of displaced food, just take a moment to imagine and appreciate where it came from.

If you live in North America, the greens in your salad probably came from a neighboring state. That beef probably came from Texas. The hops in your beer probably came from Washington State. That wine probably came from grapes in several states, most likely California. All of this has been growing for months or years, then labored over, iced, packed, and shipped on trucks over hundreds of miles. Then it sits on a shelf at the grocery store, waiting for you to pick it up and pay. Imagine how many human hands have handled your food before it gets to you. How many machine hands?

After traveling for four months, I was feeling the need to just stay put for a bit before another long road trip. That's when my dad told me about this room opening up at a USDA organic produce farm owned by a good friend in Washington. Every once in a while, we'd go visit there just to hang out and have fun — play pool with the farm folk, shoot guns, barbecue, have a bonfire, or pick some fresh produce. This seemed like an ideal place to hang out for the summer. So I jumped at the chance to help out. I was already an organic shopper, and I've always wanted to know how it's made. What goes into it? What sets organic farming apart from non-organic industrial farming? Why does the food taste better? And why do I feel better when I eat it?

The room was month-to-month, no strings attached, and it would cost less than $500 to live in harmony with nature and eat all the organic produce I want. A no-brainer. I put the pedal to the floor to get to that farm as quickly as possible.

* * *

Dharma Ridge Farms, now operating on historic Boulton Farms land, is a long, skinny strip of 200 acres wedged between the 101 and the Olympic National Forest, surrounded by miles and miles of pines and now protected as farmland and natural habitat *forever* by the Jefferson County Land Trust.

The farm is in the middle of the forest, half an hour outside the closest city, with no internet and barely any cell service. A natural stream known to run salmon brings fresh mountain spring water to the faucets and farm fields. Blackberries, plums, multiple kinds of apples, and even raspberries grow wild during the summer. Right outside my front door was fifty acres of every kind of organic produce you'd ever want/need. It also used to be a dairy farm, so the property is littered with freezers stashed with USDA Organic Grade A grass-fed beef — the best steak I've ever had in my life. Every day, I cooked a beautiful feast that I picked for free. And every other day, I juiced fresh organic produce. I ate like royalty.

Humans have been connecting over food for hundreds of thousands of years. Having lived in Italy for a while, I had already fallen in love with food not only for its ability to make my mouth orgasm, but also for its ability to bring people together. Once I'd moved in, I asked about working on the farm part-time. I didn't need the minimum-wage hourly rate; I did it because I enjoy physical labor, and I wanted to know firsthand what goes into farming the food that I eat every day.

Farming is one of the oldest and noblest professions. It's also the toughest and best work I've ever done. I'm pretty physically fit, but I was still hurting every day, especially my back. By lunchtime, I was ready for a nap, so I would prepare my lunch in the morning, then wolf down my food in ten minutes to maximize nap time. That's how tough the work was. You should have seen the owner of the farm — he was ripped!

The experience working on the farm gave me so much more respect for the land and those who create delicious things from it. I think it's unfortunate that most of us no longer have that connection to our most basic needs. Now we depend on others for our survival, and it's a crime that we pay them so little. I think every child should have a farm experience as part of their human education.

My advice: Get outside. Get physical. Put your hands in the dirt. Hunt and grow your own food. For hundreds of thousands of years, this was the lifestyle we lived in order to survive, and it does something to your spirit to reconnect with this legacy.

* * *

My experience on the farm highlighted the fact that outsourcing is a huge problem in our modern-day, on-demand lifestyle.

But we don't just outsource our food. By outsourcing everything from heat and A/C to our political opinions and even our life decisions, we are letting somebody else drive. And when you let somebody else drive, you're taking a big risk. Wherever that driver decides to point the wheel, you're along for the ride. And if they crash, guess who pays: YOU.

Why would you put your future, your dreams, or your vehicle (you) in anybody else's hands?

Even before I got rid of my apartment, there was something about the extreme responsibility of vanlife that appealed to me. I hadn't been happy with my life in Austin, Texas. But instead of complaining about it, throwing a temper tantrum, blaming everybody else, drinking away my sorrows (admittedly, I had already done all of these things in the past and had found that they weren't effective), I decided to actually do something about it. I took responsibility for myself and my life. That meant taking responsibility for the good *and* the bad. Nobody had put a gun to my head and forced me to live the life I was living. Ultimately, it was *my* fault. And I needed to make a change.

It's challenging for most of us to own up to such sober self-assessment, especially when we are so separated from the responsibility of our most basic needs. Our comfortable lifestyles have made us jaded and entitled. There are far too many people playing the victim and not taking responsibility for their own lives. Instead, you hear the usual excuses:

"It's the food companies and industrial farming that made me fat and unhealthy."

"It's the government's fault that I don't have a job."

"I'm broke because the 1% is hoarding all the money."

"It's my parents' fault I'm so messed up."

"My financial situation is my boss's fault because he won't give me a raise."

"It's all Trump's fault."

Sorry to burst your bubble, but you're fat because you choose to eat food that your body doesn't like, and you choose not to exercise. You're unemployed because you choose to stay complacent instead of continuing to learn and grow and provide more value to the marketplace. You're broke because you choose not to live below your means and save money. You're messed up because you choose to medicate with toxins instead of working through your emotional issues. Your boss won't give you a raise because you don't deserve one. And unless you're close personal friends with Trump, he has no real impact on your daily life.

Whatever it is, it may not be your fault, but it *is* your responsibility. All of it. So what are you going to do about it?

You are the driver of your life. Your current life situation is a direct result of YOU. You decide what to do, where to go, what to buy, how to make money, where to live, how much to sleep, what to eat, etc.

Your foot is on the gas, and your hands on the wheel. So stop blaming your parents, teachers, spouse, children, employer, politicians, rich people, corporations — whoever. It's time to take responsibility for yourself. When you do, life is so much smoother.

Taking a breather from life on the road gave me a chance to realize that it was my hands on the steering wheel. Nobody else had driven me there. It was me.

I was to blame for my circumstances. Or rather, it was my past self, my past thoughts, my past actions, that had gotten me to where I was. And at that moment, that made me feel really good because my life was fucking awesome! After all, I had just landed on an organic produce farm where I lived in harmony with nature in a great community of farm folk and was simultaneously working on fun projects, including my own films. I was seeing the world, making good money, and getting out of debt. It seemed that I had finally reached Destination Freedom.

Or so I thought…

DETOUR #2

Santa Fe, NM

And now for another detour from my story. A detour to one of my favorite destinations on the road…

I had been driving all day. I was tired and cranky. Pretty typical for life on the road.

I pulled into the Walmart to rest for the night. Ah, home sweet home. Time to get some shut-eye. But then I noticed the surveillance towers set up around the perimeter of the parking lot. Strange.

In my experience, Walmart parking lots had been the perfect places to stop for the night. But these surveillance towers, which looked like big light poles, were flashing bright blue lights like a cop car. Not only was this not very conducive to sleep, but it all felt very strange. Then I saw a security patrol car driving around — I'd never seen one of those at Walmart before. Was the Walmart under attack or something?

Then the patrol car started circling my van. Was I in some sort of trouble? What did I do?

I asked my technology about it, and Google helped me to discover that New Mexico does not allow overnight parking at any of the Walmarts in the entire state. Not sure why. They'd get a lot more tourist traffic if they did. But maybe they don't want tourist traffic. This is when a “Plan B” would have been helpful, but I didn’t have one yet. So I drove around for an hour or so, looking for a discreet place to park.

Finally, I found an apartment complex backed up against some nature with no parking restrictions. One good thing about not being able to finish painting the van was that its inconspicuous, plain white panels made it look like any old contractor’s van — white and plain. It blended in well. If I was subtle about it, there’d be no way to know that somebody was sleeping inside. This was, however, before I had installed any window coverings, so whenever a car drove by, their headlights would shine right in my face. I was unprepared, but it was a good way to learn. I would eventually add window coverings and a partition to keep the back of the van separate from the cockpit.

The next morning, I woke up and was having trouble breathing. I had been struggling with the altitude since Moab, but Santa Fe is almost half a mile higher. Altitude sickness is no joke. Sometimes my hands would get tingly, I’d get lightheaded, or my heart would start racing, trying to pump more blood to my organs. The worst side effects were the panic attacks, but I hadn’t had one since Moab. I went on a run downtown to get my lungs acclimated, then set up shop at the local Whole Foods to work. I felt a little better but still had some shortness of breath.

A nice lady asked if she could sit at the table across from me to get access to the Edison plug below to charge her phone. I didn’t care. I asked her if people often struggle with altitude in Santa Fe. She said it was very common, and she recommended I try chlorophyll (and, of course, Whole Foods carries chlorophyll). She told me that it works extremely well because it oxygenates the blood quickly. So I decided to give it a try.

My new friend monitored my progress for an hour or so just to make sure the chlorophyll was working and that I was okay. Very nice of her. As a side note: It’s interesting how differently people responded to me after I started living in a van; I believe it’s because one’s energy naturally becomes more open as a vagabond.

Once her phone was charged, she left with a pleasant goodbye. I went back to my work, grateful for the oxygenation in my blood. But then she came back.

"I want to give you something," she said. She dug into her bag and pulled out a business card. "I'm not sure what your plans are today, but I work at this place."

I looked at the card. It was good for one free admission to a place called…

"*Meow Wolf*?" I said.

"It's like a… interactive… permanent art installation," she said, sort of stumbling through her explanation. "Like an experiential… art... experience."

"That sounds… hard to explain," I said. "Maybe it's something you have to experience for yourself."

"Yes, exactly," she said, relieved. We were on the same page. "Something tells me you'd appreciate it."

My plans for that day had been to go to the Georgia O'Keefe museum, but because vanlife taught me to pounce on opportunities that come my way, and I had free admission to a place that was literally indescribable, I felt like I had to check it out. The nice lady bid me farewell and took off.

* * *

I drove over to the location and knew right away I was in for a treat. Outside of "Meow Wolf" were giant statues of a robot, a spider, a wolf, and a dinosaur. Kind of cool.

I went inside and was surprised to see how busy it was. There was a gift shop, a small cafe, and some bathrooms. But the interior felt much smaller than the massive building had appeared from outside.

I gave my ticket to a guy at the front desk. "Have you been here before?" he asked.

"No."

"Do you have any history of heart conditions or epilepsy?"

"Noooo…"

"Please sign this waiver."

What the heck was I getting myself into? I was even more confused when he handed me the 3D glasses.

"What are *these* for?" I asked.

"Some people say it enhances the experience."

Okay…

"I'll give you a tip since it's your first time: check the mailbox for clues."

"What mailbox?"

"Enjoy."

And he ushered me through a door. Seriously. What the hell was going on?

Inside, everything was dark. I was in a long hallway, at the end of which was a dim light. I walked toward the light. At the end of the hallway, I turned the corner to find a house. An actual house — like, a front porch, a lawn, windows, a front door, bushes, and a mailbox. No joke.

I opened the mailbox to find a letter written to me. It explained what had happened at this house after new-age experiments had been performed by the owner. According to the writer, the owner had been studying astral travel through deep meditation. Then the whole family had disappeared. The letter asked me for my help to figure out what happened to the family. All the while, hidden speakers played the sounds of crickets.

I went inside the house, and it was, for all intents and purposes… a normal house. I found notes and scientific drawings. I'm not that familiar with quantum physics, but it looked as if the owner of the house had discovered a way to not only travel to other universes, but to actually build new universes. So strange.

The whole house felt very lived in. I even went into the living room to find a stereo playing nice music. It was as if the family had just disappeared in the middle of a normal day. On the TV was some sort of infomercial about the homeowner's work — kind of like a lecture of sorts, revealing more information about his work on traveling between universes with his mind.

I went into the kitchen, and everything looked normal. Out of curiosity, I opened the fridge, hoping to find some actual food I could eat. Instead, the refrigerator door opened into some sort of tunnel… Like a *portal*.

Out of the corner of my eye, I saw another guest emerge from the fireplace. What was going on?

I started to get a trippy feeling, a bit like when you first take acid. The edges of reality were starting to fade away, revealing an entirely new reality. I stepped into the refrigerator and walked through the portal. On the other side, I found a whole other world.

* * *

I suddenly found myself on the bridge of an alien ship. Then I went through another portal and entered a blacklight forest where I found a glowing mastodon skeleton, with a xylophone ribcage you could play music on.

I found one of the kids' rooms — a child who was obviously obsessed with boy bands, where a portal in the closet took me to a similar kids' room in a parallel dimension. But this one looked like it would be Jack Skellington's son's room from *The Nightmare Before Christmas*. The deeper I went into the house, the more it morphed into something else. And it kept going and going and going. There must have been about a hundred of these rooms containing other universes. I was on an interdimensional journey to other realms.

What is this place?!

Three hours later, I emerged back into the real world, still with no idea what I had just experienced. That said, Meow Wolf was just as my friend had described: an interactive… permanent art installation... storytelling… art… experience.

Outside, I actually ran into her as she was on her way to start her shift.

"Oh, hi!" she said. "So, did you enjoy it?"

I didn't know what to say. I'm not sure I said anything. It was hard for me to tell if I was actually back in the real world yet. *Is* there a real world? I felt like I was tripping on drugs.

I found Janüs. I touched it. I put my key in the lock, and it unlocked.

Okay. Yes, this is real.

Never in my life have I experienced anything like this. It was like doing drugs, without the drugs. In fact, I had to smoke some weed just to come down from it. Wow! How had I never heard about this before?

A few months later, Meow Wolf was featured in *Rolling Stone* magazine, *The New York Times*, NPR, and even a feature-length documentary about this new category of entertainment experience and its origin story. The world was finally discovering Meow Wolf. But I was lucky enough to have experienced it before it became a thing — for free!

Keep yourself open to new experiences and opportunities. A random conversation with a friendly woman led me on a trip through the multiverse. Who knows where *your* journey will take you?

Chapter 19:

YOUR GAS AND BRAKE = YOUR SPEED, TIMING, RHYTHM

Big Sur, CA — September 2018

I had reached Destination Freedom. And so, as any explorer would, I planted my flag in it, declaring it mine. Then it was time to go further.

After staying in Washington State for the summer, I was ready for an even bigger adventure. This time, it was a cross-country trip to Florida for a professional storytelling seminar that I had strategically booked as far away as possible. I could have attended this seminar in Nashville or SoCal, but I wanted to give myself the ultimate cross-country challenge to test my van abilities. I planned a six-week itinerary, crisscrossing the country to see all the places I had always wanted to see. I knew it wouldn't be easy to be on the road that long, but I had no idea what I was in for...

I headed down to San Diego first, wanting to experience the historic CA-1. And for the record, I can now say I've officially driven every inch of the CA-1.

I ate at Nepenthe restaurant, which I had wanted to visit for a while. It's a famous restaurant on the cliffs of Big Sur, but I was mostly interested in it because Orson Welles had once owned it. Unfortunately, there was not a single thing I could order on the menu because of my dietary restrictions. It took me fifteen minutes to custom-order something pieced together from all corners of the menu. It was pretty expensive, and the food was just all right. Really disappointing after how long it took me to get there. But the waitress was very nice and helpful. (She was kind enough to tell me where her daughter usually gets her marijuana if I wanted some. But no thanks.)

After I gorged myself, I went to visit Pfeiffer Beach to see Keyhole Arch. I chatted with the park ranger when I arrived to try to get more info about the arch, who informed me that the sun only sets through the arch during the winter. This was a little disappointing, but I still wanted to see it. And unfortunately, it was super windy that day, and the purple sand on the beach was being picked up and thrown at my hairy legs. This stung like tiny little acupuncture needles, so I didn't stay long.

I was about to leave when I decided to ask the park ranger for some suggestions on where to park overnight, knowing that state park areas are usually pretty strict about this. But before I could even finish my sentence, she interrupted me. "You can park here," she said.

What?!

"We keep tabs on the beach overnight, so as long as you pick up after yourself and promise to be respectful, we can keep an eye on your van for you," she said. "And we'll be back here at 8 a.m. to open the gate."

Wow! What an offer.

"Well… I really appreciate that!" I said.

I decided to take pictures of Keyhole Arch in the middle of the night because you see so many pictures online of the sun setting through the arch but none of it at night. There wasn't a cloud in the sky, so I figured it would be a good night to see the stars.

I went back into the park to do my evening routine, watch a movie, and go to sleep, but not before setting my alarm for midnight so I could hike out to the beach with my camera equipment. The results speak for themselves.

***

California Highway 1 is no joke.

There are no speed limits. No cops. No cell service. The roads are rough, bumpy, archaic, and not very well maintained. And it's windy ... *very* windy. I had to tie everything down in the van so it wouldn't fall over and break while constantly shifting gears up and down hills and pulling 180-degree turns on the edges of sheer cliffs with no guard rails, no shoulders — no safety net. And for some reason, this is bicyclers' favorite place to train?

Not only is the CA-1 some technical and dangerous driving, but it's common to encounter drivers who aren't paying attention because they're constantly looking at the beautiful views, driving ten to fifteen miles an hour under the speed limit on straightaways. Can't blame 'em! There are hundreds of stunning unmarked beaches with white sand, turquoise water, and tons of natural rock arches.

On a particularly high and technically demanding cliff-side pass, a lady in a Prius in front of me couldn't handle the pressure. The speed limit on straightaway sections of the CA-1 is usually set at 55 mph. But on the windy cliffs, it's impossible to go that fast, so people go whatever speed they're comfortable with. This lady was apparently comfortable driving 15 mph, unconcerned with the long line of cars behind her. But instead of honking, I just flashed my brights to remind her that there was a line of cars behind her, and legally, she was required to pull over to let people pass. She passed several turnouts before she finally understood and stopped to let everybody pass.

Driving the CA-1 is not for the faint at heart. But it's worth it. Even I found it to be a pretty intense experience. But this is the sort of place where I thrive. And fortunately, a Ford E350 Super Duty 5L — even loaded down with a house inside — can haul ass up a hill. A bigger engine means a heavier payload, which means kick-ass suspension, so I was passing people left and right. In one stretch between San Francisco and Big Sur, I passed a dozen cars in a row.

At that time of year, the temperature was in the 70s, with not a cloud in the sky. There were cute beach towns, great seafood places everywhere, quaint little coves, fishing villages, inns, B&Bs, resorts, the occasional mansion, and about a hundred state and national parks and campgrounds. There were, however, very few gas stations. But this wasn't a problem, as for some reason, my gas mileage was sky-high. I went almost five hours on about a quarter-tank when I usually get six hours out of a full tank.

Despite the beauty, after a few hours of the same beaches, cliff overlooks, turquoise water, crashing waves on jagged rocks, and natural arches... it gets boring. It's best to just focus on the dangerous driving at hand. If not, you're bound to fly right off one of those beautiful cliffs and die.

* * *

Ever get frustrated getting stuck behind somebody? Whether it's a line of a dozen cars or just one overly cautious lady in a Prius, you're bound to encounter drivers who will slow down your progress — if you let them. Luckily, on the highway of life, there are usually multiple lanes going your direction. The question is, do you prefer to take the slow lane or the fast lane?

The slow lane is more congested with people who want to stay safe and comfortable. This is usually the nine-to-five route: doing what you're told and going with the masses. This isn't necessarily a bad thing, as there are advantages as well as disadvantages to driving in the slow lane. You fit in, a community is easy to find, it's safer and more secure for families and children, and it usually comes with a consistent paycheck. But you're not in control. Once you commit, you're stuck there for the long term, and your lifestyle is in control of you.

I call this "lifestyle servitude," in which your main purpose becomes *maintaining*. Your responsibility is to maintain a job or a certain level of income just to pay for the lifestyle you've grown to be dependent on, which may not be very fulfilling. Your life is not in service to you; you are in service to it.

The only way out is to switch lanes into the fast lane. Here, it's less congested, so there is less competition and more opportunities, but you have to be conscious because your fellow commuters travel gut-wrenchingly fast. It's more dangerous, *much* scarier, and more exhausting. Things are also less certain and less comfortable, so the fast lane is not for the faint at heart. But that also makes it more fun and exciting! There are lots of surprises in the fast lane.

As you may have already gathered from the title of this book, I like to live life at 70 mph, full speed ahead, pedal to the floor, hang on to your hats, fellas — always on the move, split-second decisions, too many things to do and see, too many people to help. Go, go, *go*!

I was made for this shit! The fast lane is where you grab the wheel and haul ass to your dreams.

So what lane are you in?

How fast do you want to go through life? Do you want to relax and take your time to enjoy the scenery, or do you want to ride like hell to experience the most you possibly can? You choose.

What's the speed limit for the road you're on? Careful! Travel faster than the speed limit, and someone's bound to have a problem with you. Or you risk getting into an accident because your speed doesn't match the rest of the traffic in your lane.

But, then again, what fun is it if there isn't a little risk involved?

After clocking untold hours on the road, I can vouch for the fact that the faster drivers usually get first dibs on opportunities like exits and openings. They're traveling through space and time more quickly, therefore decreasing the amount of time it takes them to get to that opportunity. When a spot opens up in a prime lane, the faster driver is there first; their momentum makes it easier to slow down than it is for slower drivers to speed up. In this way, the faster drivers have more control and, therefore, prime placement for opportunities.

But let's take this analogy one step further. We all know that faster driving decreases your vehicle's fuel economy. The same is true on the highway of life. If you never slow down, you'll tend to get burned out more quickly. The more momentum you have, the easier it is to make quantum leaps — but the harder it is to slow down and relax.

For those of us who aren't interested in spending our lives in the slow lane *or* burning ourselves out to the point of exhaustion, there is hope. Because progress isn't always dependent on speed alone. Rather, your timing and rhythm play an integral role.

Have you ever noticed how some drivers seem to get through traffic so much more easily and efficiently? They ride the waves of traffic like a savvy investor rides the waves of the market — buying and selling at the right time so they benefit in up markets and down markets alike. Yes, the type of vehicle (body) and engine (mind) you have does help, but it's mostly about being in the right place at the right time.

Luck is what happens when preparation meets opportunity. So how do you control it? By being proactive and offensive, staying aware, and maintaining control. It's about using the gas *and* the brake to control your speed strategically, slowing down and speeding up at the right times.

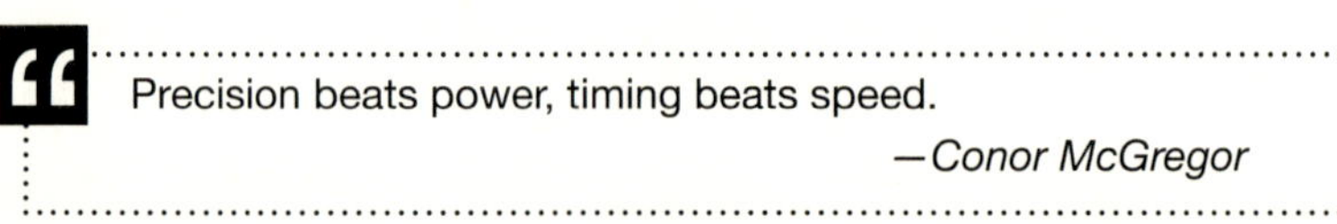

Precision beats power, timing beats speed.

—*Conor McGregor*

* * *

Waking up in the morning on Pfeiffer Beach, the location of the world-famous Keyhole Arch, was pretty amazing. I mean, how many people get to do that? Talk about timing! If I hadn't arrived at the beach at that exact time and chatted with that exact park ranger, it probably would never have happened, no matter how fast I was trying to get there.

After my morning meditation on the beach, I did my journaling and reading, followed by exercise and, finally, a jump in the cold water for my shower. Then I drove to the next beach town to do the same thing all over again.

I was settling into a groove: Sleep where I could hear the waves. Wake up on the beach. Morning routine seaside. Swim in the ocean for my shower. Work at a local coffee shop. American breakfast or protein shake at noon, then on to the next place. Once I arrived in a new beach town, I found the nearest nature to go do some hiking and take some pictures. Then grab dinner at an ocean-to-table restaurant with some local fish and wine. I usually found the local movie theater after dinner. And then, you guessed it, go to sleep where I could hear the waves. And because I was in control of my speed, some pretty awesome things came my way.

At a place called Glass Beach, I spent my morning routine with the wildlife — a daring, fat squirrel came to drink from my teacup but startled himself when he accidentally tipped it over. At Pudding Creek, I swam with a sea lion who popped up out of the water like, "What the hell are you doing here?" And in Fort Bragg, a nice young lady paid for my morning tea, which I sipped on the beach while doing my morning writing.

Despite the slow drivers, my trip down the CA-1 was probably my favorite part of the entire van journey. You might say I had reached my optimal speed, and it was smooth sailing.

How do you determine your optimal speed? This is the speed at which you are in FLOW, where your skill level is perfectly matched to the challenge of the task at hand. Time seems to warp, you lose yourself, and everything around you seems to fade away. Things work smoothly and effortlessly.

We all have an optimal speed. Janüs the van, for example, just happens to have an optimal speed of 70 mph. (How lucky is that?) Any faster, and he starts shaking. Things get uncomfortable, fuel efficiency drops dramatically, he's hard to control, and components break down more quickly.

Maybe you're the most comfortable working a nine-to-five lifestyle and taking weekends off to relax, explore, or rejuvenate. Maybe any faster than that and you get burned out. That's okay. But you can raise the ceiling of your optimal speed through maintenance and health. Take

good care of yourself, exercise, eat well, and be more strict about sleep, and you'll find that you can thrive at higher speeds than you're used to.

What is your optimal speed? You owe it to yourself to find out.

Chapter 20:

REST STOPS = REST AND RELAX

Santa Barbara, CA — September 2018

My endurance had finally reached its limit.

Living life at 70 mph is always go, go, go, which makes relaxation time even more important. But how do you relax when a van is all you have?

Picture this. It's early evening. You've worked for a few hours this morning at a coffee shop in the middle of nowhere. You've been driving for five hours, with a stop in the middle to explore a cool site just off the side of the road. Now, you're about to arrive in the city where you plan on spending the night. You're starving, so you grab some quick and dirty road food. You're tired, cranky, and trying to digest crappy food. But it won't be dark for another couple of hours.

All you want to do is have a drink to relax, sit, and veg out in front of the TV, but you have no place to go and nothing to do. Nothing's stopping you from relaxing in your van. But it's kind of cramped and hard to fully stretch out and relax. And if you're trying to keep a low profile, you don't want to be seen just hanging in your van in a parking lot for hours.

So what do you do?

You can go to a bar and drink, but doing that every day can be expensive and wildly unhealthy. You can go to a coffee shop, but they usually close at five or six. You can hang out at a restaurant, but you'd better have something to do to pass the time — and you'd better tip your waiter nicely if you plan to hang out there for hours on end. Nature is a good option, but unless there's a convenient place where you can park and sleep, it doesn't always work out... Can you see how these daily logistical challenges would start to get exhausting after *months* on the road?

As my adventure continued, movie theaters became my sanctuary. They're quiet, private, and dark, and films are hypnotic and relaxing — they turn off your frontal lobe and allow you to settle down without falling asleep.

Movies can get expensive, of course, but at that time, I was a member of a subscription service that allowed me to see one movie per day for free for only $20 a month. (It used to be MoviePass, then Sinemia, but both companies have since gone out of business.)

My movie habit proved to be such great medicine for me, allowing me to completely forget about my troubles. And while movies might not be what *you* need to destress while on a pitstop from the highway of life, you've got to have a method of relaxation that you can rely on.

Whatever method you have for decompressing, it is important to understand the value of rest and relaxation, especially when you travel.

Travel can be tiring, causing significant wear and tear on your body, so you'll need even more time to rest than usual. This makes it more important than ever to make sure you schedule time for R&R, or else it may not happen.

Regular relaxation is much easier to implement when you have a daily routine. So whatever your routine is, make sure it includes R&R.

Chapter 21:

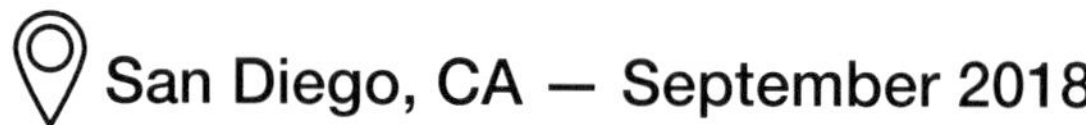

HEADLIGHTS AND REARVIEW MIRRORS = PRESENCE

San Diego, CA — September 2018

We're now about halfway through this account of my vanlife journey, and odds are, if you're still reading this book, then you've probably gathered that my life up until 2018 hadn't exactly been smooth sailing. And in September of 2018, my travels took me back to one of the rockiest stretches of road in my life: my childhood.

We'd all like to believe that our existence was planned as a result of a strong bond of love and companionship between two consenting adults, thus thrusting us into this wonderful world with safety and security, protected by two loving parents working together as a team to raise us in a loving and supportive household.

But in most cases, life is much messier.

One could make the case that this is the more natural origin story, anyway. After all, life on this planet evolved out of a fiery, volcanic, unstable, volatile environment — the farthest thing from stable and safe and secure. Humans tend to thrive in chaos. And my childhood was no exception.

The circumstances of my birth still mystify me. Seven years before I came into this world, my existence was predicted. At the time, my uncle was married to a highly clairvoyant individual. One day, she and my uncle came over to my dad's place for dinner. When my dad opened the door, my aunt was frozen in the entryway, staring stoically at a point directly above my dad's head.

"There's a blonde child hovering over your head. He's wondering what's taking so long," she said like a zombie. (Anyone who knows anything about me will know that this *had* to be me, since I am known to be incredibly impatient.)

My dad thought this was strange. Neither he nor his wife at the time was blonde. But, lo and behold, a few years later, my dad ended up getting divorced. He later moved to San Diego and met my mom. And not long after that, they had me.

Apparently, my aunt even told my dad all about me and the circumstances of my life. She said that the two of us would be unusually close for a father and son, and that I would "influence many people." Most of the details she shared ended up being accurate, especially about my birth — that something would go terribly wrong at the end but that I'd be safe and healthy. Just as predicted, on the day of my birth, I had meconium while still in my mom's uterus and was born with the umbilical cord wrapped around my neck. But despite the complications, I ended up being fine.

I was a pleasant surprise, but my parents tried to make it work on my behalf. I have fuzzy memories of lying in my crib, hearing yelling in the other room. To this day, I hate when people yell. It was a rocky start, and in the end, it just wasn't meant to be for them. They split up when I was only a year old.

Eventually, it was decided that I would live with my mom for the first half of my childhood (until I was nine years old) and then live with my dad for the second half. In reality, I was being moved back and forth between two single parents constantly, and it didn't help that they were moving around all the time.

In order to save money for a down payment on a house someday, my dad was usually either renting a cheap apartment in a bad part of town or renting a room in a co-op house. And half the time, my mom couldn't afford a place of her own, so she was either living with a boyfriend or renting a room out of somebody's house. In both scenarios, I often didn't have my own space and had to share a room or bed with somebody — in somebody else's house! I never had a place I felt I could call "home."

And I was never comfortable. When I was with my mom, I was unattended most of the day because she worked all day. She would drop me off at daycare an hour before school started, then pick me up around dinnertime. And because I wasn't getting enough attention, I sought attention by causing trouble. So much trouble that I knew the principal personally. I saw him on an almost daily basis.

I had a lot of pent-up anger from being left alone so much, and since it was difficult for a "problem child" like me to connect with kids my age, I retaliated by hurting my peers. Getting in fights and throwing rocks at other kids. Fortunately, sports were a healthy outlet for me — I loved kicking butt at handball, soccer, and karate.

Needless to say, I wasn't well-liked. But I was fine with that because I never really liked or understood my peers anyway. They weren't the ones I longed to connect with; it was my parents who I needed.

"I had a shitty childhood." A tale as old as time, right? More like an excuse.

My "shitty childhood" became a story that I told myself for my entire adult life. I blamed my mom for it. But the truth is, I always got the worst of her because I usually only saw her at the end of the day when she was tired and cranky. All I remember about her from my childhood was yelling, anger, and the word, "NO!" I felt like I never got what I needed from her emotionally. And as a result, I never had any respect for her. We didn't see eye to eye, we didn't understand each other, and our relationship was one of constant tension.

Once I moved in with my dad at nine years old, everything changed. He bought a condo right down the street from my school, and he was home all the time because he worked from home, so I always had somebody around. I changed overnight. I became well-behaved. I changed my circle of influence, stopped getting in fights, stopped getting sent to the principal's office every day, and became a straight-A student.

With my mom, it was constant conflict. But with my dad, I had the security I needed and was able to thrive — even though it was just him and me.

* * *

Fast-forward to 2018...

Driving down to San Diego, I knew I'd be seeing my mom. And since all this stuff was coming up, I wasn't exactly looking forward to the visit.

I already knew what was going to happen: I wouldn't be comfortable at her place because she was still renting a room out of somebody else's house, which meant I wouldn't have my own space. I'd be crabby, and she'd be defensive. Invariably, something would come up that would turn into an argument. She'd get upset, and that would make me upset, and down the rabbit hole we'd go. Then it would be annoying the rest of the time I was there. That was our routine.

On the way, I called my dad to try to get some clarity. I had to understand.

"What happened?" I asked him. "Why did you guys break up? What were the circumstances of my childhood?"

As the sights zoomed past my window, I heard my dad's remorse for the first time. He was calm and logical as he explained the reasons why things had happened the way they did. I also learned that he was grateful that everything had turned out well in the end, even if it hadn't been ideal. Despite everything, I had turned out pretty great.

It was clear that Dad had longed to provide a better environment for me to grow up in, with one cohesive family unit under the same roof. But, alas, this simply could not happen between him and my mom. I can't imagine how that must have felt for either of them.

So, that answered that. But I wanted to know how my mom felt about the circumstances of my childhood.

"You'll have to ask her," Dad said.

So I kept driving. And after a few more miles, I worked up the courage to call her.

"Hey," she cooed into the phone.

"Mom," I said flatly.

I wasted no time but got right down to it. And, to my surprise, I got a completely different story from her.

According to my dad, my mom was the only person he had ever wanted to have kids with. She was "traffic-stopping" beautiful, he told me. But despite this devotion, my mom said that she felt she couldn't depend on him. I guess there are always two sides to every story.

For a while, I remained determined to get to the bottom of this. But after going back and forth with them a few times, I finally gave up. There was no way to determine what had actually happened. Who was right? Who was wrong? Who was to blame? I would never know. But obviously the answers wouldn't have solved anything anyway. After all, that had been thirty years ago. What was done was done. So I had to decide for myself.

My conclusion: It's not easy being a single parent.

My mom and dad were simply doing the best they could with what they had at the time. And my childhood was the inevitable result of my mom, my dad, and me all existing together. There was nobody to blame. Whatever happened, happened because it was the only way for it to happen. And in a way, this incredibly simple realization was yet another step toward Destination Freedom.

* * *

For so long, I had held on to the stories I'd told myself about my mom: My childhood sucked, it was terrible, I hated it, a kid should never be raised that way… And it was all my mom's fault. I was *attached* to my story for some reason — attached to the identity of a poor kid who overcame the setbacks of a shitty childhood. Like it was a badge of honor or something.

Janüs the van helped me realize that this story wasn't serving me anymore. It wasn't serving my mom, and it wasn't serving our relationship.

Family was super important to me, and I didn't want to have that kind of relationship with *any* family member, let alone one of my parents. It was unacceptable to me. So I decided to let go of those stories, forgive my mom, and focus on what I appreciate about her.

Turns out, my mom's a pretty rad lady. (Probably one of the reasons I'm so rad.) She's super creative, fun, and social. She's a rebel, she's strong, and she don't take shit from *nobody*. She's a great cook. She makes me delicious gluten-free, dairy-free treats. She knows how to have a good time, and she always takes care of me. I can call her anytime, and she always wants to listen and help. That's real love. That's unconditional love. How could I deny that?

My childhood is the reason I am who I am today. Without that experience, I wouldn't be me. I wouldn't be so strong, so independent, so emotionally intelligent, so street smart, so charming, so good with people. So it was time to write a new story.

I decided I was going to share my revelation with my mom. I wanted to let her know that I was sorry that I had blamed her for so much and that I had finally forgiven her. I planned to have this talk with her when I arrived in San Diego. And I was not looking forward to the conversation.

I felt like I already knew how she would respond. She never likes it when I talk about my childhood because she sees it so differently. I felt that no matter what I said, she would take it personally and get hurt and upset. Then it would turn into an argument, and blah, blah, blah.

Mom and I went to the Bernardo Winery and drank some delicious wine. Surprisingly, my visit was rather pleasant this time, not tense like it usually is. I never saw an opportune time to share my new outlook with her. It just didn't seem appropriate, and the last thing I wanted to do was ruin one of the nicest visits I'd ever had with her. So I decided it was better that I didn't say anything. After all, this was a decision I had made for myself. Maybe telling her wasn't necessary.

But then something amazing happened. When I left San Diego a few days later, there was a long email in my inbox. It was from my mom.

In the email, Mom shared with me her dissatisfaction over my experience of my childhood. She apologized for not being able to provide the environment that I felt I'd needed as a kid.

I couldn't believe it. Somehow, she had subconsciously sensed a shift in my energy toward her. That was why the visit had been so pleasant. Because I had changed; I had forgiven her. And thanks to that shift, she had shifted, too.

I called her from the road again. We spent a couple of hours on the phone talking things over, and it was very healing. Now I call her from the road all the time. I know she likes to get updates from me. The phone is one of her love languages, and she feels loved when her kids call her. These days, we have a really awesome relationship, and I enjoy my time with her immensely.

Eventually, my dad let go of his guilt about my childhood, too, and he felt free. My mom even sat down with him alone at one point to tell him that she wanted to get rid of the anger she had toward him. This was anger she had been carrying with her for over thirty years. He told her that he had no ill will toward her and was happy to help her do that in any way he could. Apparently, there was some important healing that occurred between them. I like to think it was a result of my inquiry. Now they have a great relationship, and they talk frequently.

* * *

Living in a van makes you extremely present. Most days, I don't even know where I'll be sleeping that night, let alone where I'll be living next month. Or where my next paycheck will come from. If it's a long trip, I'll have a few weeks of destinations and friends planned out, but the details are discovered in the moment. Translation: You have no choice *but* to be present. And in that extreme presence, I find peace.

I used to be wrapped up in the stories of the past, like my difficult childhood. And I was constantly worrying about the future. But living in a van has shown me what a waste of time that is.

Our time is limited, so why waste it? It doesn't mean you shouldn't use your mind to learn from the past, but there's no use in allowing it to absorb you.

Break free so you can live your life now!

Picture yourself driving up a mountain at night. You can't see anything in your rearview mirrors because it's dark. You can't even see much of the road ahead. All you can

see is just a few feet in front of your headlights. So, where do you look? Your awareness remains within the illumination of your headlights: no further than what's right in front of you.

Your immediate future is before you. Yet so many of us live outside of the present, putting things off, trying to focus on a far-distant future that we may never even live to see. That's why so many people put off the things they want to do until retirement. And tragically, for far too many of us, life runs out before that mythical "someday" ever arrives.

Instead of waiting for your retirement later, the vanlife allows you to live your retirement NOW. Instead of "someday," you're acting in the present moment. You are creating your life in real-time. It's instant, and it becomes easier to see it clearly when you're living life at 70 mph.

The universe is responding to your energy in real-time, so be conscious of your thoughts, emotions, words, and actions. Spend less time worrying about the future, and let go of your past. Otherwise, you'll never be able to move forward. And you can't keep your eyes on the road if you're constantly looking in your rearview mirrors. That's a good way to ensure that you'll crash. You may not like what happened in your past, but you can't do anything about it. You can only change the meaning you derive from it, and that is done in the present.

Chapter 22:

SHARE THE ROAD

Estes Park, CO — September 2018

Do you feel lonely at times? Life on the road can be lonely, which is not conducive to mental health.

Driving through Colorado, one of the first places I wanted to visit was Columbine High School. As I mentioned in a previous chapter, I was interested in the subject of school shootings as research for a script I was writing.

Visiting the campus was eerie and illuminating. This script was forcing me to examine and confront my own loneliness, and studying the Columbine massacre, it was easy for me to see how young high school outcasts could get to a point where they feel that the only tribe they could possibly belong to was the growing tribe of school shooters. But the initiation into this tribe is deadly. It's scary what loneliness can do to the human spirit. And it's even more terrifying to realize what a person is willing to do when they feel like all else is lost.

My relationship with loneliness started long ago. After finishing my first feature film, I wanted to escape the busyness of Los Angeles, so I moved to a tiny town in the middle of the woods, several hours from any major city: a magical place called Port Townsend on the Olympic Peninsula of Washington state, surrounded by the Olympic Mountains and Olympic National Forest.

Port Townsend is a retirement community of only 10,000, so there weren't many driven young entrepreneurs like me. Being social was extremely difficult. And dating? Nearly impossible. The young professionals I did meet were people I just couldn't connect with for some reason. In no time, I felt very much like an outcast — as if I weirded everyone out for some reason.

As an artist, I tended to isolate myself at times, to my own detriment. I would lock myself in my house in Port Townsend for days at a time, with no contact with the outside world until I needed to go grocery shopping. I began having anxiety attacks, something I had never experienced before. Eventually, I learned that they were due to a lack of human interaction. So I developed a habit of going out to eat at restaurants just so I could talk to a waiter or waitress. Unfortunately, this was an expensive solution. After about a year of living on my own in the woods, I had become angry, addicted, disillusioned, and starving for connection with other human beings.

As I mentioned in Chapter 12, there's a reason that prisons use solitary confinement as a punishment tactic. Cruel as it is, it's effective because humans are social beings. For hundreds of thousands of years, we've been working together to survive, glued to our dearest friends and families (even the ones we don't like). I've witnessed firsthand the devastating effects of social isolation, and I've seen how easily it can lead to mental illness, depression, and thoughts of death in the form of suicide and homicide. It's the worst pain I've ever felt.

Every creature on the planet understands the power of safety in numbers. But now we live in boxes by ourselves, go to school/work in cars by ourselves, and sit at cubicles or desks by ourselves. The only real community we have nowadays is the forced association of school or work, with people who aren't necessarily like-minded individuals.

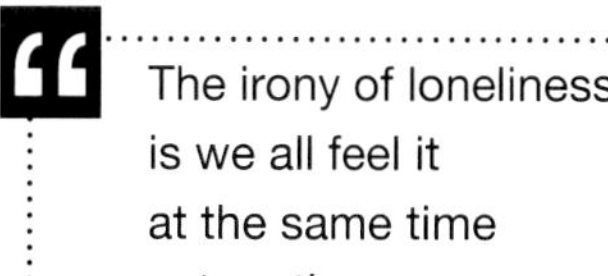

> The irony of loneliness
> is we all feel it
> at the same time
> —*together.*
>
> —*Rupi Kaur*

Get out and meet people. You're a social creature, and you need interaction, whether you like it or not.

* * *

After visiting Columbine, I went to Estes Park, where I hung out with elk, hiked the Rockies, watched the sunrise from 14,000 feet, and explored the iconic Stanley Hotel. This beautiful hotel is said to be haunted by a chambermaid who was nearly killed in an explosion in Room 217, and who eventually died after working at the hotel her entire life.

Room 217 also happens to be the room Stephen King occupied on the last day of the hotel season before winter took hold of Estes Park. That night, he had a dream about his son being chased down the hallway by a fire hose. The dream was so disturbing that he was startled awake and couldn't sleep. He stayed up the rest of the night smoking cigarettes, and by morning, he had the story outline for what would become one of his most famous novels, *The Shining*. The book eventually became one of the most deeply disturbing films ever made, starring Jack Nicholson and Shelley Duvall and directed by cinema master Stanley Kubrick. Perhaps it's no coincidence that the film (which portrays a writer who goes crazy and tries to murder his wife and son) is a commentary on the dangers of isolation.

That night, I also had a dream. I dreamed that I approached a dark doorway just like Room 237 in the film *The Shining* (they changed the door number for the movie). I intuitively knew that the doorway led to death, nothingness, the darkest depths of the human soul. But I told the doorway that I wasn't afraid, and I asked it to show me the darkness. It opened and let me in.

Inside, it was so dark that I couldn't see anything. I was alone, and all I felt was loneliness. It was a terrifying void of sadness and pain. My takeaway: To be truly alone in the universe is the worst possible pain. But after a moment of pain, there was NOTHING.

And suddenly, it clicked!

I realized that this was where these school shooters wanted to go: to *nothing*. They are in so much pain from social isolation that they just don't want to exist anymore. Yet again, pain and adversity proved to be the catalysts for bringing me the answer.

* * *

Life on the road is challenging and lonely, but I forced myself to meet people, talk to people on the street, and make friends with strangers. In other words, I learned to come out of my shell. I had never been very social before. But now, I had a reason to connect — my own survival and mental health.

I knew that the next weeks on the road would need to be planned very strategically if I was going to keep my mental health intact. I needed nature, I needed adventure, I needed friends, and I needed to stay grounded.

Denver, CO — September 2018

Like it or not, one of the most important considerations when it comes to life on the road is MONEY. How the heck do you make money on the road? Well, there are many ways to do it.

Some people have savings that will allow them to travel for long periods of time. Some have severance packages. Some have inheritances. Some own businesses or properties that give them passive income. And others have retirement and social security. But I'd say that most people who choose to live their life on the road are mobile entrepreneurs, also known as "digital nomads."

A digital nomad's work isn't location-specific. So as long they have access to Wi-Fi, they can work and make money from anywhere. As a video guy with a network that spans the country, I fall into this category. In fact, the more traveling I do, the more work I tend to get. Because the closer I am to you, the more incentivized you are to buy from me while I'm in town.

By September of 2018, my bank account was running a little low. My focus had shifted to travel and experience, so I hadn't worked in several months. But I needed money to fund my travels. So, while on my way to Colorado, I posted on Facebook asking for any connections in Denver. I shared that I was saving money to fund my travels, and I would be happy to drop my prices by HALF and kick back a few hundred bucks to anybody who could make a connection that turned into income.

My post led to a connection with a couple of guys who owned a CBD company. I met them at their booth at the local shopping mall. They were very nice, charismatic guys who were interested in a long-term content marketing contract for their social media. But, as it turned out, they mostly just wanted to know how content ought to be done, and in the end, no deal was made. Oh well. It was time to leave Denver and head to the next destination.

But about an hour outside of Denver going southbound on the I-25, I got itchy — in my mind and in my heart.

I couldn't shake this aversion to the thought of being broke on the road. I didn't want to go into debt and start using a credit card, although I was prepared for that as a last resort. So instead of feeling bad about it, I picked up the phone. Luckily, the CBD guys answered.

"You're interested in a lot of video work," I said. "So I'll tell you what. I'm leaving Denver right now, but why don't I stay in town one more day. We can shoot a short video telling your story. I normally charge four thousand per video, but I'll do this for a couple grand. Just to show you what I'm capable of. Then, based on that experience, we can decide if it'll work for a long-term contract. I really like what you're doing, and I want to help. So what do you say?"

And wouldn't you know it? They said yes. I took the next exit and headed back to Denver.

The next day, we shot some great stuff. They paid me half up front for shooting, and I edited the piece on the road. They loved the end result and gladly paid me the other half. And even though it wasn't a massive payday, that money covered my travel expenses for a while longer. I didn't even have to use that credit card.

Not only that, but my gusto was so attractive that I landed a long-term contract with them. A few months later, they hired me to shoot a few dozen videos and set up their whole content marketing system and web presence, which required me to stay in Denver for a while. They were kind enough to put me up in a nice apartment in downtown Denver, right above a Whole Foods (I love Whole Foods!).

After living without a permanent home for so long, staying in such a nice place was a luxurious dream. I felt spoiled. But I worked my ass off for them.

* * *

Money is just one of those things. You either love it, or you hate it.

Most people seem to have a rather unhealthy relationship with money. For a lot of us, no matter what we do, there never seems to be enough. Living month-to-month, paycheck to paycheck… I was the same way. But once I got my relationship to finances in order, the van became a money-making machine.

Initially, I just thought of the van as something fun to do for a while. I didn't understand at the time how valuable it would be in relation to producing a measurable return. Beyond the great memories, stories, and growth I experienced, I can honestly say that Janüs was one of the best financial investments I've ever made. The ROI was exponential. But don't take my word for it — the numbers speak for themselves.

First, let's look at my initial investment.

- The van cost me $4,000, plus the beautiful, sparkly blue rally car I traded it in.
- The build itself cost me around $8,000.
- So, in total, the project cost me $12,000, plus a few months of rent while I was building full-time.

But hold on. The financial benefits don't stop there. Because living in a van has saved me about $24,000 per year in overhead, rent, bills, etc. (You probably already know how hard the average person has to work to make $24,000.)

Okay, okay, let's be clear here — travel *is* expensive. And road food is, too. So while the van resulted in a large reduction of expenses, my new lifestyle meant that for a while, I was just about breaking even. It wasn't until I really got the hang of things and stopped traveling quite so much that the van became a money-making machine.

I still work while on the road, so I continue to produce income while I travel, but I have almost no expenses. In 2020, for example, I only grossed about $55,000, but I saved $20,000. I put $5,000 in my Roth IRA (which grew to $7,000 by the end of the year), $6,500 in an emergency account, and saved the rest for taxes. Not bad!

Perhaps more importantly, in addition to being a great financial investment, the van also allowed me to be omnipresent and to visit clients all around the country. And I soon learned that when a video guy is standing right in front of you, with all his equipment in a van and ready to go, it's much more difficult to say no to video work. My call to action went from, "Contact me if you ever need anything," to something with a snappy sense of urgency: "I'll only be in town a few days at most, so get it while you can."

* * *

As an artist, there have been times in my life when I have tried to avoid the financial cycle of production/consumption entirely. And, to a certain extent, Janüs was certainly an escape from the rat race. But now, I simply accept it as part of life.

It's like investing in the stock market; you have to learn to accept the occasional correction and fluctuation. For example, I went into debt to be at the Illuminate Film Festival in Sedona, but that experience led to work in Pasadena and Chicago, which got me back out of that debt. My trip to Washington put me in debt, too, but that trip led to farm work — and client work at Orangetheory Fitness. My trip to Florida put me in debt but led to the contract with the CBD company in Denver.

By the end of 2018, I was about $5,000 in debt, which maxed out my credit card. But by getting recognized as a traveling filmmaker, I eventually landed a $25,000 contract that not only got me out of that debt but also paid for the entirety of my travel expenses for the following year.

Now, before you decide to leave *your* life behind and pursue the lifestyle of a nomadic filmmaker, I should mention that I've been making films since I was a kid. I've spent decades building up my skill level while also building my network. This allows me to have complete control of my income. I can go and get money whenever I need it. Tomorrow, I could drive out to the middle of nowhere in South Carolina and convince a small business in need of marketing materials to pay me $2,000–$4,000 for a valuable video that would take me a few days to finish, which would then fund my travels for another month. And I've continually done this to fund my travels. This is completely different from living "paycheck to paycheck." And prior to making this incredible journey, I never would have thought that such a lifestyle was possible.

The money is nice. But beyond the financial advantages — looking at a triple or quadruple bottom line — Janüs enabled me to see the country, commune with nature, improve my mental and physical health, deepen my connections with my friends and community, make new connections, lessen my carbon footprint, grow tremendously, garner some death-bed memories, and get to know myself better. And that ROI is immeasurable.

Like it or not, money is the fuel that gets you to your dream destinations. So what's your relationship with money?

Living the vanlife certainly changed my relationship with money — and the way I earn income. Now, instead of "getting paid," I *create* money. I used to be attached to the need for MORE. I never had enough because I was stuck in a deficit mindset due to constant bills and expenses. Living in a van changed all that. Now, when I need money, I just go out and get it.

Of course, not everybody has this capability. And that's the point: My relationship with money is unique, and so is yours. Whatever associations you have with money, you'll never gain control of your finances until you reconcile your relationship with it.

Instead of seeing money as a burden, try to imagine it as the fuel to fund your dreams. Everybody wants to be rich.

But what does that mean? Money cannot be the end in itself; it must be the means to that end. So use it for what it is meant for: to fund your dreams. This simple shift in your relationship with money can make your financial life much easier and less painful.

Chapter 24:

GETTING PULLED OVER = BREAKING THE RULES

El Paso, TX — October 2018

El Paso has the distinguished reputation of being a hot, smelly, depressing shithole. So why would I want to go there? Because that's where my mom's family is, and they're pretty awesome.

I stayed in El Paso with my cousins in a house that the family owned. Fun little side note: Apparently, the previous owner had committed suicide. Where? In the room where I was staying. Oh, is that what that big red stain is on the ground? Hmm...

After a few days of shooting guns, blasting fireworks, drinking margaritas, and eating Texas-style barbecue, it was finally time to leave. But it had been many years since I'd driven through El Paso, and I had forgotten that there was a border patrol checkpoint just outside the city limits.

There is some gray area with these border patrol checkpoints. Legally, they can't stop people to ask questions or conduct random searches. It's unconstitutional. But there are a couple dozen of these checkpoints all along the border. Supposedly they allow themselves to bend the rules a bit within 50 miles of the border for the sake of our nation's security.

The chances of going through a checkpoint like this one while there's an active canine unit on duty are pretty low. But I just happened to drive through during one of these rare instances. Bad luck for me. And for the record, I don't recommend driving cross-country with drugs. But, hey, I had my entire life with me.

As I approached, I saw a dog sniffing around the cars.

Okay... I told myself. *Just stay calm. I'm sure nothing is going to happen.*

I was in such a good mood from visiting my family that the danger didn't seem real. But as soon as I rolled up to the officer, the dog barked.

"Pull over to the left here for me," I was instructed.

Now having a slightly harder time remaining calm, I did as instructed.

"Step out of the car for me," he said.

I did as I was asked. Soon, they had their dog running through my van, sniffing around.

At some point, I realized I was just letting them do whatever they wanted without really considering my rights, so I decided to speak up. "What is this all about?" I asked.

"Canines are trained to sniff out narcotics and explosives," said the officer. "The dog signaled, which means he smells something, so we're just doing a routine check of the vehicle. Standard procedure."

It all sounded so matter-of-fact, the way he said it. Business, papers, numbers. No big deal.

"We got a positive," one of them said.

Into his radio, he said, "We got a 23-19. Over." Then he turned to me. "Come inside for a sec."

Oh boy.

* * *

The border patrol officer sat me down on a cold metal bench next to a handcuffed hippy-looking kid with long hair and a long beard, then went off to push some papers or something.

As I waited there, I witnessed what I could only assume was an interrogation of some kind. Out of some back room, they brought another hippy-looking girl, handcuffed, with a red face and runny mascara. She didn't look very pleased. After they sat her down, they grabbed the dude next to me and dragged him back to the same room. I wondered what these two had done to deserve such treatment. I assumed that they'd been snagged for the same reason as me, but they didn't look threatening to me at all. Just a young couple on a road trip who wanted to party and have fun. And there I was, sitting on the same bench, nobody watching me. I didn't even have handcuffs on me.

"So why am I here?" I asked the agent at the computer.

"You're being arrested for possession of narcotics."

"Oh!" I said. "Interesting."

I was more surprised than worried or upset. I really didn't think it was that big of a deal. After all, I didn't have an employer who would care. I lived in a van, for crying out loud.

I sat back down. Nobody was detaining me even though I was being arrested. The whole situation felt very strange. So I kept joking with the agents just to make conversation. I was bored! Soon, I had them laughing.

This was my introduction to Texas's zero-tolerance law. This was the United States Border Patrol, a Federal agency, which meant that in their eyes, the plant was a Schedule 1 Controlled Substance to be seized. They didn't really care about some kid with a few nugs of pot. They were looking for illegal immigrants.

Finally, they pulled me to another computer station to be processed. While I was getting my fingerprints taken, the officer caressed my hand ever so sweetly.

"You have such a gentle touch, Agent Turner," I told my gloved captor with a smirk.

What an idiot I was. But I was being sincere, I promise.

His buddy, Agent Vasquez, then asked me, "Have you ever been arrested before?"

It almost sounded as if Agent Vasquez was second-guessing their decision. As if he was confused as to why they were arresting such a charming young man. I guess they were used to people hating them when they make arrests. Instead, I smiled.

"No," I said and shook my head in disappointment. "If I had, I bet it wouldn't be this much fun."

They both laughed. Okay, my charm was starting to work.

I was actually pretty fascinated by the process. I'd never been arrested before, so this was good research. Maybe I could use the experience for a film someday. That said, I'm aware that my experience was atypical. I was clearly being treated differently than the other detainees.

Think about it: Why do celebrities get off so easily when they get themselves in legal trouble? Because they're loved. I was probing to see how far I could go with my wit. I obviously wasn't a threat and was being completely cooperative — even cracking jokes with them. (Have you ever tried treating a cop like that when you were being given a ticket? Maybe you ought to try it someday.)

Agent Vazquez looked down at the computer screen, puzzled. "Did you call the DEA?" Vazquez asked Turner.

"Yeah," Turner replied, and followed up quickly with, "No," as if to answer Vasquez's next question.

Hmm...

They were now speaking in code and barely acknowledging my presence as they struggled to make sense of whatever they were seeing on the computer.

It took a total of four agents to process me, and halfway through, just as they were about to take my mugshot, agent Turner called over another agent for help — Agent Lee. He showed Lee the screen and pointed as he went down an unseen list, saying, "Negative, negative, negative, negative... What should we do?"

They both shrugged.

Finally, Agent Lee gave me back my wallet. "Thanks for your time. You're free to go."

As I walked to my car, I saw the canine unit sitting patiently with his handler on the side of the road, panting happily. That dog, of course, had no idea what he was doing. I guess he was off-duty, taking a break. Or maybe he'd done his day's duty and was now heading home to the bitch and pups. In any case, none of the vehicles going through the checkpoint were being checked by canine units. If I'd driven through just a minute earlier or a minute later… What were the odds? But you've got to hand it to him. He did a good job.

"What a good boy," I said, reaching out to pet him. "Want a treat?"

"Stay away from the dog," I was scolded.

Oh, jeez. Sorry.

I sparked the engine and got back on the road.

* * *

Overall, this little brush with the feds was actually a fairly pleasant experience, despite having my stuff basically stolen from me. (They didn't just take my pot. They took the entire bag it was in, which contained objects of sentimental value, not just paraphernalia.)

Was I really arrested that day? I don't know. Do I have a record now? I have no idea. Did I get a ticket to appear in court? No. Will I someday receive something in the mail? I still haven't.

My guess is that either something they saw on my record — or didn't see — got me off the hook that day… or maybe they were just fucking with me. I wasn't who they were looking for, I was pleasant and cooperative, and I wasn't a threat. It's not really the Border Patrol's job to arrest American citizens for possession of narcotics, and I'd only had a small amount. Plus, it probably didn't hurt that I went in with the advantage of being white, educated, attractive, and well-spoken. Others aren't so lucky. Still, I like to think my jovial attitude was more influential than my skin color. Maybe I just wasn't worth their time. Who knows?

But therein lies a very important lesson.

I come from a long line of rebels and rule-breakers, starting with my great-grandpa Crank, who ran moonshine in Arkansas. I've never liked rules. And rules have never liked me.

As far as I'm concerned, nobody can tell me what is right or wrong. Only God can do that. So I was a wild child, constantly out and about, doing questionable things in the middle of the night, hiking, adventuring, taking pictures of abandoned buildings — and garnering unwanted attention from skeptical authorities because my limitless attitude scared them. I still break the rules every day, even as a contributing member of society. But we're never punished for breaking the rules; we're only punished for getting caught.

The thing is, sometimes you have to break the rules to get where you want to go, especially if it requires taking the road less traveled. Sometimes you have to disobey the road signs, cut corners, and go off-roading. Life is too complex for black and white. There's always a gray area because there is no right or wrong. There is only here and now. The universe is limitless and infinite and never works within bounds or restrictions.

In my experience, breaking the implied rules of society often means that you're doing something right. Especially the rules of our culture — go to school, get good grades, get a job, buy a house, go into debt, get married, have kids, etc. "Follow these rules," they say, "and you'll be happy!" Pssh — yeah, right! Check the scoreboard. If that's the case, then most of the most impactful people in history were HUGE rule-breakers. And they don't look unhappy to me.

Breaking the rules of the legal system is a different story. In my opinion, if breaking a rule doesn't hurt or impede anybody else, then no harm is done, and there's no reason to get in trouble.

I run red lights, I drive over the speed limit, and I do illegal drugs. I admit to it. Arrest me if you want. But my actions do not prevent anybody else from living their best life.

Is it really worth the trouble of convicting me? Is that really a good use of law enforcement's time? I haven't gotten heat from the justice system because the answer is *no*. They have more important things to do.

I've been called to the principal's office many times. I've had the cops called on me many times. But when I'm confronted by authority, for some reason, they tend to let me off with a warning. To me, this only further proves the insignificance of the rules.

I know it sucks to get pulled over, and it sucks to get in trouble. I hate it when authority figures treat me like I'm a horrible person just because I make an illegal U-turn. But I know I'm not a horrible person.

Fear and shame are simply control tactics. If they control your emotions, they control you.

As soon as the border patrol agents saw that they could not control my emotions — and that I was actually pleasant and making the experience enjoyable despite the fact that my life could have become much more difficult with a felony on my record — they dropped the act immediately and forgot the role they were playing. This allowed us to relate to each other as humans again. And we laughed.

Why do cops seem so hateful and angry when they pull you over? Because they get so much hate and anger directed at them. It's natural to get scared or angry when you've been pulled over, and most direct those feelings at what they consider to be the source of their pain: the officers who are just doing their job. That's car-ma (car karma). You receive what you put out. And I believe that karma comes around. Not eventually, but *immediately*. Instant car-ma.

So, coppers, do whatever you need to do to get your job done, but there's no way you're going to affect my mood and make me feel bad about myself. I will not allow that. Instead, we're going to have fun during our little business interaction. I'm in control here. There's a new sheriff in town.

With that attitude, not surprisingly, I haven't gotten a single ticket since I moved into the van. I've gotten pulled over many times but I've never gotten a ticket. Now that's car-ma.

Sometimes you've got to break the rules to get to where you want to go. But if you're not hurting anybody, don't worry about it! Just don't get caught. And if you do, take the chance to connect with the authority figure in question. Treat it as the business transaction that it is and try to have some fun in the middle of it. This person is just doing their job, so why not connect as human beings?

If you put out good energy, you receive good energy pretty much across the board, consistently, every time. If you have good car-ma (car karma), there's nothing they can do.

CHAPTER 25:

YOUR ENGINE = YOUR MIND

New Orleans, LA — October 2018

In the beginning, I thought vanlife would just be a fun thing to do for a year. It took me about six months before I really began to see the benefits of what I was doing. This wasn't just a fun experience. It was a new and more empowering way of life.

In October of 2018, I found myself at a bachelor party in New Orleans with a bunch of friends from Cutco (the direct sales company I used to work for) who really wanted to see the van because they had heard so much about it. And I love showing people the van because I enjoy seeing their reactions. There's always somebody who says something like, "Oh, I've always wanted to do this." And, sure enough, there was a guy — I think his name was James — whose eyes lit up as soon as he saw Janüs.

"OMG, I respect you so much," said James. "Because I've always wanted to do this."

"Same here," I replied. "That's why I did it."

And I've always wondered... If these people are so interested in doing something like this, why don't they just *do it*? Later, when we were all hanging around the campfire, James kept asking me question after question about the van. It seemed as if he were seriously considering the vanlife. So finally, I just asked him point-blank, "If you really wanna do this thing, what's stopping you? Why don't you just do it?"

His answer blew me away.

"I feel like I have to build something first," he said. "I feel like I have to achieve some amount of success or money before I deserve to or can allow myself to do something like that."

Suddenly the veil was lifted for me, and it all became clear.

I immediately saw all the pieces of programming that we subconsciously download as children: I saw how James had been conditioned to believe that he wasn't worthy of his dreams and wouldn't be until he accomplished certain things. Simultaneously, I saw that all these pieces of programming were being deleted from my mind one at a time. Things like...

1. Go to school
2. Get a job
3. Buy a house
4. Go into debt
5. Save/tithe/invest
6. Retire at 65
7. Then enjoy your life

For thirty years, I had been told that *this* was how life worked. But the vanlife had effectively purged this belief system from my brain — thirty years of programming erased in less than a year on the road.

The vanlife wasn't just about traveling anymore. I was beginning to see the tremendous life-changing impact it was having on me. Back when I'd first decided to take the leap, I could never have anticipated the extent of what it would ultimately mean to me.

* * *

There are certain "truths" that we take for granted. And in hindsight, I can see that for my first thirty years on this planet, I'd been force-fed someone else's idea of what life should be.

I had been told that there was only one way to live life: get a degree, get a job, buy a house, get married, have kids, go into debt, live below your means, and save/tithe/invest. And then, fifty years later, I was allowed to retire and finally reap the rewards of my hard work.

So I followed the program perfectly. I got straight As. I won trophies and awards. I earned three scholarships and two degrees and graduated magna cum laude. I learned a marketing skill that was valuable to the economy and I made enough money for a nice place and fancy car. From an outside perspective, it would appear that I had followed the rules to a T, done everything right, and gotten everything that would make me happy — or at least what I was told was supposed to make me happy.

Even though I had "it all," I'd still felt unfulfilled. That, of course, had been the impetus to leave my old life behind. But I hadn't understood the full extent of what had brought me to that decision. I now realized that I had committed the worst sin of all: **I had become what everybody else told me to be, rather than being me**.

The difference between me and someone like James was that instead of complaining, feeling powerless, or getting angry and playing the victim, I had decided to actually do something about it.

Sitting around that campfire, I could see myself in these guys (at least, the self I had been six months prior). I'd been there. Stuck in that rat race. My purpose on the planet was reduced to making money just to pay my bills. I could see for the first how much I had changed since I started living in a van — how different I was and how much I had grown. And it wasn't just in relation to money. My relationship with EVERYTHING had changed.

Yes, the van was a vehicle that I used to drive through my life to Destination Freedom. But it wasn't just freedom from a job and bills and debt. It was freedom from the web of false beliefs that had imprisoned my mind and kept me chained to a system that I didn't even enjoy. Because, just like James, I had been led to believe that there was only one way to live life. Only one road to Destination Freedom. And that lie had been the worst imprisonment of all.

* * *

> Give me a child until he is seven, and I will show you the man.
>
> *–Aristotle*

For the first seven years of your life, your brain was working overtime to map the world around you. This was when you learned everything you needed to know about how the world worked and how to survive in it. Concepts like career, money, education, groceries, housing all took form in your head.

Over the course of these early years, I had downloaded all the programs I needed to survive. It wasn't until I started living in a van that I witnessed my programs changing.

1. HOUSING: Instead of living in a house with bills and a mortgage or rent, I lived in a van with no bills and no debt.
2. MONEY/WEALTH: Instead of having a job, I created money wherever I went. I learned that life was about being rich in EXPERIENCE instead of being rich in money and material possessions.
3. INDEPENDENCE: Instead of working for somebody else, I worked for myself.
4. LOCATION: Instead of staying in one spot, I traveled everywhere. And instead of being inside all the time, I was outside in nature constantly, developing a stronger connection to the natural world.
5. PRESENCE: Instead of thinking about the future constantly, I lived completely in the present. Instead of waiting for my retirement later, I was living my retirement NOW. And instead of waiting for a magical "someday," I acted in the present moment.
6. RELATIONSHIPS: Instead of seeing the same people over and over again, I met and connected with new people every day.
7. FREEDOM: Instead of being tied to a system, I became completely free from it. And instead of doing what I was told, I created and controlled my own reality.

And those are just the top seven that come to mind. Living in a van magically cleared my old programming. I'm committing to writing my own programs from now on, thank you very much.

The engine is the mechanism that allows the car to drive. But *your* engine is not your feet or your legs or even your heart. It's your MIND.

Your beliefs and programs are what drive you. So, what programs are you running? You don't go to college because it's the best thing for you — you go because you *believe* that it is the best thing for you regardless of whatever debt you may incur. You don't get a job because that's the best option for you — you get a job because you were conditioned to *believe* that steady employment is the path to money and happiness. You were likely taught that there was only one way to live life. And yet, that's the biggest lie of all, because human creativity is limitless.

There are literally infinite ways to live your life. You can make money in any number of ways, or not make money at all. You can live in a house, an apartment, a hotel, a campsite, a van, an RV, on the street, or any combination of those options. You can live in any city, anywhere, or you can choose to never wake up in the same place twice. And once you get out of your shell, you can find community anywhere, do anything, and be anybody.

Your life is a great work of art, and you are the artist.

In my old life, I wasn't a human being; I was a human DOING. The purpose of my life had been to *do* something every day to get money.

Most people feel they need to *do* the actions/behaviors they think will allow them to *have* the stuff they want, which will then cause them to *be* happy. I thought that if I worked hard running a business, I would get a bunch of money, and therefore the freedom to make my own films. Then I would be happy. But, like most people, I had it backward. So, once and for all, here's the real secret formula to happiness:

You must be the person you want to be *first*. Doing this will attract the people, opportunities, and tools you need to *have* in order to *do* what it is that you want to do.

Living in a van brought me back to a human *being*, in which the purpose of my life was to simply be 100 percent me. The van gave me the freedom to be my wild, adventurous, creative self so I could have the time and space to focus on what I wanted to do: make my films. Doing what I loved every day not only made me happier but also attracted into my life more filmmaking opportunities.

Living life at 70 mph was kind of like getting unplugged from the Matrix. All of a sudden, I saw the code, and I was unplugged and reprogrammed. The traditional production/consumption lifestyle suddenly seemed like a prison to me. And it's hard to step back inside a cage after you've learned to see the bars.

Keep your mindset in check. Will your programming take you to where you want to go? Some people want to be rich, but they carry around a deep-seated belief that rich people are greedy and evil. Hmm... With that belief, you'll never become rich (unless you want to be greedy and evil). So it's time to change your thinking. Others just want to be happy, but they think that it's the fancy lifestyle that will make them happy. Happiness is a feeling that comes from inside. So if you rewrite your programs to have the power over your mind and emotions to feel happiness regardless of the situation, then you will invariably attract the fancy lifestyle you want.

If your programming is off, you may not have the horsepower necessary to get up those mountains. If your programs aren't serving you, rewrite them! Give your engine a tune-up — it brings a whole new meaning to the term "street smarts."

Chapter 26:

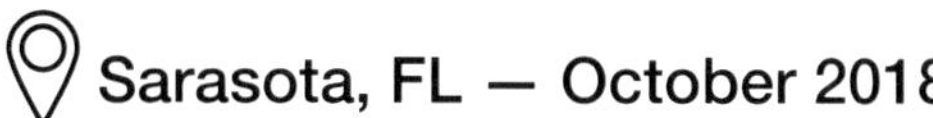

BLAZE THE TRAIL = LIFE IS A STORY, YOU ARE THE WRITER

Sarasota, FL — October 2018

In October, I finally got to Florida! But it was a little different than I expected. (Life usually is.) And I wasn't just there for the beautiful beaches. I had paid to attend a storytelling seminar by legendary screenwriter Robert McKee.

As I cruised into Sarasota, I suddenly realized it was October 18, which would have been my late grandpa's 100th birthday. This was very special to me because his presence had been instrumental to my development as an artist. My talent came from him, and he helped me along the way in many ways. It was like he was there at the storytelling seminar with me.

The next day, the seminar began. I learned a ton about storytelling, but I was surprised to learn much more about humanity. I believe I grew as a human through those three twelve-hour days, sitting and listening to McKee's lecture. I had to swim through a sea of personal opinions and diatribe to get the value, but overall, the content was indeed very valuable. I learned more about myself and my gooey, mushy insides. I am human, after all — flawed, emotional, and filled with my own fears, desires, and beliefs.

My biggest takeaway was the nature of the storyteller's job. Namely, that there is a problem in contemporary storytelling: It mostly sucks. Why? Because humans lead remarkably comfortable lives today with little effort.

Humans have always existed in a state of constant conflict. Conflict is a part of our nature. Even right now, looking at this text, reading these words, you are in conflict somehow. The problem is that the American way of life is *easy*! People used to have to work hard all day just to survive. But today, without the conflict of man vs. nature — the great need to survive — where did all that conflict go? I think it went inside.

We now live in a state of great inner conflict. Contemporary human conflict is existential conflict. The question has shifted from *how* do I exist to *why* do I exist? Now that survival is taken care of for us, we have been made into human resources to keep the system going. But why are we here if not to live?

For millions of years, our daily purpose was to hunt, to get food, to make shelter, to avoid the cold winter seasons... Now our purpose is to work for money. This is why storytelling is so important today. Storytelling helps us *make sense out of life*.

Storytelling is a social responsibility. Storytellers have no responsibility to be politically correct and no responsibility to cheer people up. We have only one responsibility: to convey *the truth*. All storytelling expresses why and how life happens the way it does so we can make some sense of this craziness.

In school, we learn how to do what we're told, how to memorize useless facts and figures, how to navigate social politics, and how to perform on tests. But LIFE is the ultimate test. And the screen (or the page) is the biggest classroom there is. It's where kids learn the truth about life and why it is the way it is. This is why I make films.

After the seminar, I didn't know what to do with myself. I had climbed challenging mountains, steered around obstacles, tuned up my engine, and finally arrived at my destination...

What now?

What do you do when you arrive at your dream destination? Now what? Well, make sure to enjoy it first. But then... Give back! Blaze a trail and show others the way so they can learn from your success. This is how we progress together as a species.

We're all trying to get somewhere. For so long, I just kept trying to get to the next destination, without ever just stopping to smell the roses, enjoy the view, or appreciate what I had. At some point, the satisfaction of accomplishment wears out. But that's when you begin to truly appreciate the journey.

You are the hero of your own story. But you are also the writer. So what story do you want to tell? And what is your "character" here to learn?

For me and my character arc, I thought my adventure with Janüs the van would be an epic hero's journey with crazy struggles along the way that would push me to grow in the unexpected ways needed to reach my final destination. I was right. But I couldn't put into words what I had learned or how I had grown.

Little did I know, this was not my final destination. And there was still much more for me to learn.

Chapter 27:

Altamonte Springs, FL — November 2018

There I sat, on one of the most beautiful white-sand beaches I had ever seen. It was like something straight out of a magazine. Turquoise water, palm trees lining the boardwalk, bikinis everywhere. The sun was perfect — not too hot, not too cold.

I had the perfect morning. I woke up on the beach, meditated while the sun rose over the water, and did yoga on the grass. Florida was turning out to be everything I'd hoped for in my van adventures: paradise.

But I wasn't happy at all.

The constant travel had taken its toll. I was exhausted mentally, emotionally, physically, and spiritually. My credit card was finally maxed out, and I was down to my last five hundred real dollars. I had no work prospects, and I was living on the streets in a hot van, completely and utterly alone.

I thought I had hit rock bottom before, but this was a new record low for me.

This was probably the most difficult leg of my journey. It's difficult for me to share the dark experiences I'm about to relate to you, but I'm not going to lie about my situation or pretend that my vanlife was picture-perfect just to appear higher in some imaginary social strata.

I felt the need to stay in one spot for a bit to get grounded and relax, so I stayed in Florida by myself. I was supposed to have some work waiting for me there, thanks to a Facebook post that had gained a few positive responses. Four people in the area had replied to say that they wanted some video work, and two others had indicated that they were interested. But, one by one, each of these opportunities fell through for one reason or another — bad timing, out of town, moving, budget, money problems, whatever.

I've been doing client work since high school, and work seems to follow me wherever I go, but I wasn't used to losing that many sales. I was ready to do work, but nobody wanted any help from me. What was going on? Was it me? Maybe my energy wasn't agreeable. Maybe I was just done with life. I was so exhausted. I needed a break.

I made the most of my newfound time and freedom by working on some personal projects that really excited me. Previously, I could never seem to find time for my personal projects, but taking a break from traveling all the time freed up a lot of energy. I wrote for at least eight hours every day. I hadn't been that prolific in years.

I found a nice new development with a scenic lake, a Whole Foods, and a movie theater all within walking distance — a magical place called Altamonte Springs — and those few weeks in Florida, though challenging, actually became a very creatively fulfilling time for me. Still, with no friends, no family, and no clients, I was really lonely. All I had were the Whole Foods employees, who got to know me very well (probably too well).

* * *

For a while, I basically lived at the Altamonte Springs Whole Foods. I woke up every morning about half an hour before the sun rose, did my morning routine in a nice courtyard on the water watching the sunrise, did some yoga or ran around the lake, and then went straight to Whole Foods to write. I wouldn't stop writing until around 5 p.m., when I had dinner from the hot food bar. Then I would go catch a movie to wind down and do it all over again the next day.

"You must live nearby somewhere," someone finally asked me.

Not surprising that they would take notice of me, considering that I literally sat in the same exact spot in Whole Foods every single day, seven days a week.

"Yes, right around the corner, actually," I admitted.

Literally... In a van in the parking lot!

Living inside of a grocery store has its fair share of temptations. I became addicted to collagen coffees, dairy-free ice cream, those little chocolate almond butter cups, Bulletproof bars, and cheap Japanese saké. Frankly, it was an amazing lifestyle, but I didn't have much privacy, didn't have anywhere to relax other than the movie theater, and slept in a hot van at night (so hot that I would sweat nonstop and wake up dehydrated). This would have been an ideal time to get an Airbnb for a few days just to decompress, but I had no money.

I knew I was in trouble when homeless people started talking to me. There were three individuals in particular who would regularly come by and visit me at my spot in Whole Foods to say hi and chat. I've spent a lot of time with personal growth junkies, so I'm very familiar with the Jim Rohn adage that "you are the average of the five people you spend the most time with." No judgment whatsoever, but I have to say, hanging around those homeless people was not the most elevating company. But I was desperate for human interaction and tried to see it as an opportunity to elevate those around me.

But hold on... *Elevate* those around me? What made me think these people *needed* to be "elevated"?

It gradually dawned on me that I saw myself as better than these people. But how was I any different than them? I, too, was homeless. I, too, had no friends. I, too, had no money. I had become one of them, and they could tell somehow.

Homelessness is a strange feeling that is difficult to describe. I felt like I was hiding something and was embarrassed at the idea of anybody finding out my secret, which caused me to distance myself from people, even though I desperately needed that connection for my mental health. It was lonely, scary, sad, and depressing, yet strangely comforting.

In a way, I felt special and unique because I was so different from the others shopping at Whole Foods in their yoga pants. But I felt *too* different. I started to believe I'd never be able to truly connect with anybody because there was too much distance between our lifestyles. I felt broken, as if there was no hope for me. I had no schedule or responsibilities, which was very freeing, but I simultaneously felt imprisoned in a deep dark hole that I had dug myself. It was the most bizarre duality I had ever experienced.

This was my situation, like it or not. Vanlife isn't pretty sometimes.

I spent a lot of time exploring the nature of these feelings. In the process, I gained a lot of respect for homeless people and how they live. It's so challenging, demeaning, and demoralizing — I have read that homelessness can even cause brain damage. And I feared that the same was happening to me.

At my lowest, I reached a point where I no longer felt human. Whether or not you give some change to a homeless person, at least treat them like the humans they are. Don't ignore them. They do exist.

* * *

There was one bright spot amid the hopelessness I felt during those dark days.

Whole Foods is such an incredible health haven that they even have massage chairs for all the busy moms running around doing their errands (perhaps they need it most). The masseuse was there Wednesdays and Fridays, so I kept seeing her around. She caught my eye — just something about her.

Eventually, I worked up the courage to get a massage from her. I asked her for her number, and we went on a walk around the lake for what she referred to as "our first date."

A few days later, she didn't show up at the massage table at her usual time. I texted her. She was stuck in bed with a migraine so debilitating that she couldn't even go to work. So I brought her some good marijuana I scored from one of the homeless guys I met. We hung out and chatted while she smoked the joint I rolled. Then I asked her if she needed me to leave so she could rest.

"Honestly, it feels much better when you're here," she said, trying to muster a smile through the pain.

I massaged her shoulders to see if that might help more blood flow to her brain. But once I began touching her, it was game over. She started to move in ways I can't even put into words. And I melted. I massaged her earlobes. I stroked her eyebrows, caressed her cheeks, and kissed her on the forehead where the pain was. She purred and turned around to kiss me. Her tongue was soft like velvet. I tried to turn her around to face me, but she wouldn't let me leave her mouth. I guess she needed me just as much as I needed her.

I hadn't been inside an actual human home in almost a month, so I needed to accomplish some domestic tasks. Needless to say, I got a shave and a shower and I felt like a new man.

In our intimacy, I shared with her my struggles with loneliness. Biologically, we need face-to-face interaction and safe/secure intimacy with trusted friends/family, but she seemed to revel in her aloneness.

I didn't get it. Why were others enjoying themselves while I was writhing in pain? I hated it.

"Are you happy when you're alone?" she asked me.

And that got me thinking… No! I am not happy when I'm alone.

I can't just sit and relax. I was constantly running between my morning routine and my writing and the movies and dinner, behaving as if I was super busy even though I really had *nothing* to do. I felt like I had to be doing *something* just to distract myself from the heavy feeling of this black hole in my chest.

Hmm… So why would someone who is unhappy being alone go on a solo road trip and purposefully isolate himself?

* * *

Almost entirely by accident, I had stumbled upon a major incongruency between my feelings and my actions. Had I done this vanlife thing for all the wrong reasons? Had I confused wanderlust with loneliness? By running away from my self-isolation back in Austin, had I actually isolated myself even further?

My friendly masseuse pointed out that perhaps the reason I was so lonely was that I wasn't comfortable spending time with myself. But why? *Is loneliness an issue of self-acceptance? Do I not like myself?* WHOA! Talk about a loaded question. I have self-love and self-acceptance affirmations that I say to myself daily — I was sure I *liked* myself. So maybe I was just disappointed in myself.

Looking back, it occurs to me that I did have old friends outside of Orlando. I could have easily reached out for help and crashed with them for a bit. I had plenty of frequent flyer miles — I could have flown somewhere else to be with family. But I wasn't allowing myself to do that; I felt like I didn't deserve it. I just wanted to sit in the dirty hole I'd dug, like I was punishing myself.

I was disappointed in myself because I felt that I had failed — failed at getting work, failed at this whole van thing, failed to get to the Keys, failed with money because I was broke, and failed at my relationships because I had nobody. I was still exercising every day, so at least I had my health, but I was eating a lot of junk food (as junky as you could get at Whole Foods, at least). And despite being as straight-edged as a born-again Christian throughout my travels up until now, in my agony, I had started smoking and drinking again. And I even felt like I'd failed society — I was no longer contributing to anything except Whole Foods' P&L.

Coming down from the high of a nine-month van adventure traveling the country, I felt like I had reached the lowest point in my life.

Where am I? Where'd I come from? How'd I get here? And where am I trying to go?

I was so lost. And eventually, my bank account reflected my emotional state.

Finally, I ran out of options. My only choice was to use my miles to fly back to my dad's place in Washington with my tail between my legs. I didn't even have enough money to get an Uber from the airport to my family's house. The whole experience was so embarrassing.

But I still tried to search for the silver lining. Living in the van, I had learned a *ton* about the true meaning of life. I'd gotten to know myself deeply, and I'd rid myself of some old programming that was no longer serving me. I saw the whole country! I saw things that I could never have imagined! I fell in love with myself! And I experienced memories that would be with me on my death bed. For crying out loud, it was one of the best experiences of my life. It had been overwhelmingly positive. But… I was exhausted from the constant go-go-go. So I was happy to finally be taking a break from the vanlife, to get some R&R, to take some time to work on my projects, to process what I had been through, and to spend time with my family.

I wasn't super happy to be going back to my dad's place, but none of these benefits would have been fully realized if I hadn't failed *forward*. That's how we learn and become better versions of ourselves. I had grown tremendously (including experiencing some major growing pains). But my muscles were sore, and I needed time for them to recuperate and repair.

I wonder why progress looks so much like destruction.

—*John Steinbeck,*
Travels with Charley: In Search of America

What do you do when you take a wrong turn and find yourself lost? Do you sit on the side of the road and mope like I did? Or do you stop and read the street signs?

What street are you on, and where are you headed? The street I was on was surely headed to a destination of drug addiction and homelessness. Do you reach out to loved ones and ask for help? Do you take out your map and try to regain your bearings? Do you run away and avoid the feelings? Or do you face them head-on?

Whatever you do, don't give up. You don't ever really fail. You always gain *something*.

CHAPTER 28:

GETTING TOWED = ASKING FOR HELP

Port Townsend, WA — November 2018

I left the van safe and sound at "The Magic Estate," a big brick castle at the end of 7th Street in Orlando, where a bunch of magicians lived with a dolphin trainer.

Yes, you read that right. A castle full of magicians and a dolphin trainer. Life on the road is anything but boring.

The magicians were actually in the process of moving out, so they offered me all kinds of toys and gadgets they were trying to get rid of. You want an electric bicycle? You want a scooter? You want a snowboard? Anything you want, just take it! But I had made a vow of minimalism, and the van couldn't fit any of these fun items. Still, there was one thing that caught my eye and could easily fit in the van: a soft green stuffed dragon with big eyes, pink horns, and purple spikes running down its spine. I dubbed him Puff the Magic Dragon, and he became my copilot, accompanying me on every journey since.

When I landed in Seattle, I had $9 in my bank account, but my phone estimated an $80 trip from the airport to my family's home. I didn't even try my credit card — it hadn't worked since I'd pushed it over its $5,000 limit at the storytelling seminar. I hesitated before pressing the "Confirm Uber" button. But luckily, it worked. It didn't charge me until I arrived at my destination.

How the heck did I get here?

When I'd set out on this van adventure, I had known I might run into this problem at some point. I was well aware of how expensive my travel plans were, as well as the challenges involved in the lack of work coming my way. But I never anticipated that I would dig myself this deep into a hole.

Janüs was still back in Florida. And since I had no transportation, my aunt allowed me to borrow her Lexus GS hybrid during my stay in Washington. Fortunately, it already had half a tank of gas in it when I picked it up from her house. Otherwise, I would have been screwed! I zoomed through the Olympic Peninsula to Port Townsend, Washington, and pulled up to my dad's condo in style. Not a bad way to retreat. Things were starting to look up.

* * *

I've never been that great at asking for or receiving help. Being raised by two single parents, I grew up very independent. As soon as I could reach the knobs on the washing machine, I was doing my own laundry. As soon as I could light a stove, I was cooking my own breakfasts and lunches. I never needed anybody's help with anything, especially not with money. So when I showed up at my dad's place $5,000 in debt, I felt utterly defeated.

Not long ago, I was making six-figures! And there I was, homeless and broke, trudging back to my dad's house, begging for money. It was humiliating. I felt like a child, incapable of taking care of myself.

Well, that's how it felt, anyway.

Objectively, it really wasn't all *that* bad! I was only $5,000 in debt, which I knew wouldn't take long to pay off. Honestly, I had nothing to complain about. First-world problems. When you refocus your mind to appreciate what you have instead of regretting what you don't have, it's easy to see how abundant life actually is. At least I still had a car. At least I still had clothes on my back. At least I still had my filmmaking skills. And at least I still had a family who loved me and wanted to help.

When he was younger, my dad was forced to live out of his car at one point when money got tight, so he understood my situation. He made it easy. I didn't even have to ask. He offered me some pocket cash right away. He's also the one who convinced my aunt to let me borrow her car. I was so out of it that I didn't even know what to ask for or how to allow myself to receive. I already felt indebted to them for so much they'd done for me over the years. But I guess that's what you do for family. I regret that it took me thirty years to realize how lucky I was to have such an incredible family. But that's okay, because I know now.

I needed a metaphorical tow. And fortunately, there was someone willing to haul my broken self, free of charge. Why not just accept the help, learn from the experience, and move on?

We're all wired differently, I guess. I was an independent, high-achieving, decorated lone wolf with high standards. I was wired to be ashamed of the inability to take care of myself. I think we are all wired this way to some degree, to our detriment.

Socially, we give honor and appreciation to those who are already successful and wealthy — with high-paying jobs, fancy cars, and expensive houses. But maybe, in a way, we've got it backward.

Those at the top of the social pyramid already have everything. It's those at the bottom who need it most. But most people would sooner give an expensive gift to a powerful CEO in the hopes of tapping into his/her network than provide a small financial boost to a neighbor who could really use it.

We all need a tow every once in a while. We're not superheroes! Sometimes we get injured, sometimes we lose a loved one, sometimes we lose a job — there are always peaks and valleys. Perhaps it's time to learn to give

help when you're on a peak and ask for help when you're in a valley.

I had no way of knowing at the time that my lowest point was, in a way, a blessing. In fact, that holiday season was the most memorable of my life. I received so much love from the Conedera side of the family — my aunt, my uncles, my cousins, their kids, and, most of all, my dad. I had never been closer to them than I was that year. It was incredibly healing for me. That's when I realized how blessed I am to be a Conedera. I reveled in who I was and learned that sometimes, being lost is the best way to find yourself.

Chapter 29:

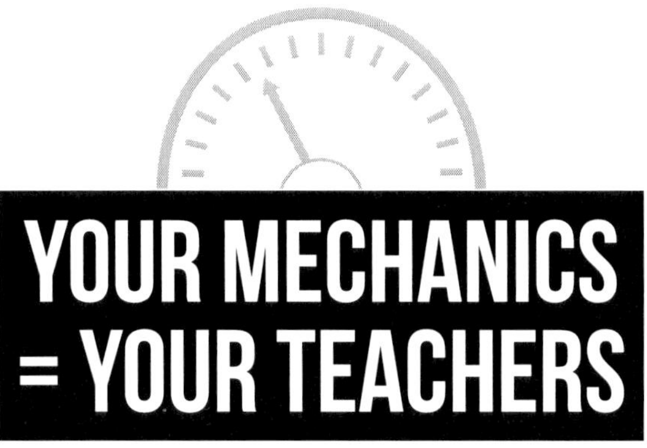

Your Mechanics = Your Teachers

Olympic Mountains, WA — December 2018

Port Townsend is a beautiful place, but it's also old, small, slow, and isolated. I've always had a somewhat tumultuous relationship with this maritime city.

I had been visiting Port Townsend every year since I was a kid because it's where my grandpa retired and died. Then my dad retired there, too. So it's always felt like home to me. But it's also where I experienced the darkest period of my life.

This was back in 2013. After realizing I hated Los Angeles, I had moved to Port Townsend, and soon after I arrived, I injured my shoulder in a soccer game with some locals. After surgery, I was isolated and taking lots of oxycodone. I had a cool house right on the water and was healing in the middle of the forest, all by myself. Port Townsend is mostly a retirement community with a population of just 10,000 and very few young people for me to connect with. Plus, I was new to the area, so it was very lonely. My only companion was Tigger.

Anybody who knew me growing up knew my cat, Tigger. She was hard to miss. A loud, orange and white calico with lots of energy and attitude, she always made sure her presence was known. She was social and constantly attention deprived, despite the fact that she got all the attention. We were inseparable. She was like a daughter to me. I loved that cat so much. Still do.

Because of the social isolation in Port Townsend, I began experiencing strange panic attacks. My heart would race, and I couldn't breathe. I felt like the world was ending. All I had to cope was good Port Townsend beer and that oxycodone. So I started going downhill fast.

I started hurting myself. Breaking things. Punching holes in the walls. The drugs and alcohol certainly didn't help, but the lack of connection with other human beings was really affecting my mental health. I actually looked forward to my painful physical therapy appointments because my physical therapist was the only person I could talk to.

That was when I noticed that Tigger hadn't eaten anything in days. And her litter box was empty.

I took her to the vet, and they said her kidneys were failing, so I should put her to sleep. But I didn't feel it was my responsibility to kill her, and I didn't feel comfortable supporting some industrial veterinarian sales scheme. Humane? I don't know. I'd let Tigger decide when she was ready to go.

I made the whole day about her, doing all of her favorite things: letting her outside to lie in the sunshine, giving her tuna water, watching a movie with her in my lap while I brushed her. I think she really enjoyed it, but I couldn't really tell because she could only take a few steps at a time before stopping and falling down.

I had read that animals like to go into dark places to be alone when they know they're dying, so I built her a death box. Basically just a cardboard box with her favorite blanket in it, which I decorated with drawings of her favorite things and my favorite memories with her. As soon as I set it on the ground, she immediately got inside. She knew.

Lying in bed that night, I wondered, *Was her life worth it? Were her last days enjoyable? Was I too mean to her?* Waiting for the inevitable, I drifted into dreamland.

I woke up at about 4 a.m., which is a time I don't normally wake up. I went to the death box to check on her. She was lying in a comfortable, relaxed position with her tail in a perfect curve around her legs. Her mouth was open. Her eyes were open, but there was no life in them. She had died peacefully in her sleep in the middle of the night.

When I picked her up, the last of her saliva fell out of her mouth onto her favorite blanket, and I lost it. I cried over her body for hours. I've never felt pain like that before.

Later that day, I wrapped Tigger in her favorite blanket and put her in my backpack. I drove up to the top of the Olympic Mountains, around Hurricane Ridge. It's a national park, so you're obviously not supposed to bury your pets there, but I was a little off my rocker at the time.

Tigger was on my back. My left arm was still in a sling from the surgery, and my right arm was carrying a pickaxe. I hiked off the trail to find a cliffside that overlooked Discovery Bay and my grandpa's house, where we lived. I found the perfect spot. With one arm, I dug a hole with the pickaxe, buried her, and had a little ceremony, reading some words from friends who knew and loved her.

* * *

Sometimes, when I'm feeling especially lost, I like to hike up to Tigger's gravesite just to meditate and have a conversation with her. Her grave is marked by a rock and three tree brothers that I like to think watch over her. So in 2018, when I was stuck at my dad's place, with no van, no money, a bunch of debt, no work prospects, no friends in Port Townsend, lost in my life, I made a trip up to visit her.

"I failed!" I told her. "Isn't that great? So, what now? What's next?"

She didn't say anything. (She never was a very good listener, but her silky smooth fur had been therapeutic. Too bad I could no longer stroke it while standing at her grave.)

I asked Tigger what she thought I should do. She didn't have much advice, so I decided to ask others.

My dad said I should get a job. My friends said I should move back to Austin. Another friend said I should make another movie. My mom said I should settle down and get married. A client said I should start another business.

Notice that not a single person said I should keep living the vanlife!

Be careful who you take directions from. Doing so is basically doing what others tell you to do, which is always risky. You may end up way off course from your original destination. Consider the source. And the credibility of the source.

One of the best ways to hack your results is to see how other drivers have gotten to where you're trying to go. If you're trying to start a charity, check out how other founders have done it. If you're trying to meet your soulmate, ask couples who've been together for more than fifty years. If you're preparing to run a marathon, study other runners and their workout routines. Entrepreneurs call it "modeling," but that's a nice way of saying "copying" or "plagiarism." It's okay. Go ahead and copy! You can even get coaching from those more experienced than you — those drivers who have already been where you're trying to go.

> Be careful who you take directions from, you might end up miles off course of where you wanted to go.
>
> —*Zig Ziglar*

* * *

When it became clear that I wasn't going to gain a sense of direction from my friends and family, as good-intentioned as they were, I turned to my heroes instead (most of whom were dead, unfortunately).

In Salinas, I visited the John Steinbeck Museum, where I got to see Rocinante, the camper-truck he lived in with his poodle Charley in the book *Travels with Charley*.

In Santa Rosa, I made a point to visit Francis Ford Coppola's winery, where he has his five Oscars on display, as well as the Tucker car from the film *Tucker: The Man and His Dream* (1988).

In Philly, I visited the Ben Franklin Museum. In the Keys, I visited the Hemingway House to see his writing room and resident six-toed cats. I enjoyed the Warhol traveling exhibit when it was at Balboa Park in San Diego. I visited the new Apple campus in San Jose, California to remember Steve Jobs and his impact on my life. In Houston, I visited Howard Hughes's grave. And outside of Paso Robles, I visited James Dean's crash site. I also visited the Chapel of Sacred Mirrors in New York to attend one of Alex Grey's events.

These heroes of mine... What would they say?

"It's not an easy destination." I turned to my left to find John Steinbeck sitting next to me. "But it's the noblest and worthiest pursuit," he said.

"Ruff!" His poodle Charley panted excitedly at his feet.

Then Ben Franklin butted in. "If you have something to say, then say it," he said, looking at his timepiece as if wondering how long this was going to take.

"Fuck 'em all, man." I turned to find James Dean leaning up against the wall in the back corner, lighting a cigarette. "You got a gift. Share it with the world."

"Let me help you," said Coppola, toasting with a bottle of his own wine.

"I really like your work, keep doing it," Warhol said to me, smirking. "You also have such an interesting face. Can I photograph you?"

Hemingway just listened, nursing a scotch, waiting for a lull in the advice-giving. His eventual response was so efficient. Just one word: "Purpose."

Suddenly, the door flew open, and a loud voice boomed, "You wanna be a filmmaker? Make films! You wanna live in a van? Live in a van. You wanna impact culture? Then make your own culture." It was Howard Hughes in aviator glasses.

"Here's to the crazy ones..." Steve Jobs said quietly.

Then the crowd of geniuses parted like the red sea, the lights dimmed, and a spotlight illuminated one tall man at the back, smiling warmly. It was Joseph Campbell.

"Follow your bliss," said Joe.

* * *

The adventures of the road had distracted me enough to cause me to momentarily lose sight of where I was going. Destination Freedom, remember? But where was that? And how did I get there? My heroes helped steer me back on course.

All the people I looked up to were innovative and prolific creators whose contributions to culture and humanity were undeniable. Often misunderstood or misrepresented, these stubborn rebels not only had immense vision but also the impractical idealism it took to *act* on their vision despite bad directions from others. That was who I wanted to be; that was where I wanted to go.

Another recurring theme is that these innovators also all had notable periods of poverty and struggle while refusing to give up their dreams. Coppola refinanced his own house to pay for *Apocalypse Now* (1979) when no studio would touch it. Ben Franklin dropped out of primary school and left Boston at age seventeen with almost no money in order to find work as a printer in New York, despite what his father demanded of him. Steve Jobs was homeless after dropping out of college and slept in the common rooms while crashing the classes he enjoyed, even though he wasn't paying tuition. James Dean couldn't rub two nickels together while living in LA trying to make it as an actor. So, by living in a van, I must have been on the right track.

But what were my dreams? Was I still going in the direction my GPS (my heart) was telling me to go?

If your engine is your mind, then your mechanics ought to be your thought leaders, your teachers, your mentors, and your heroes.

Who do you go to in order to keep yourself sharp? Who do you allow to work on your engine? These are your teachers. You can read Tim Ferriss or Deepak Chopra, you can listen to Tony Robbins or Joe Rogan, you can watch Gary V. or TED Talks. However you prefer to learn, driving is a great time to do it.

Chapter 30:

YOUR DESTINATIONS = YOUR HEART'S DESIRES

Denver, CO — January 2019

After the holidays, I flew back to Florida to pick up Janüs and drive to Denver, along with my new copilot Puff the Magic Dragon, to take that job with the CBD company. I needed to start making more money again to get myself out of debt. Spoiler alert: It didn't end up being much money at all while living a cushy lifestyle downtown, but I would manage to pull myself out of debt over the course of the following year.

They put me up in a nice apartment in a high-rise right above Whole Foods, so I didn't have to worry about paying rent. I figured I could at least learn about an exciting new industry and see what it was like to live in the Mile High City for a bit.

Based on my prior experience in Moab, I wasn't surprised to find that adjusting to the altitude was difficult at first. But with exercise, Wim Hof breathing, and coffee, I was able to adapt pretty well.

A friend came over one night with a DMT pen. I took a couple of hits, and suddenly, I was in the jungle. The window blinds became giant palm fronds shading me from the bright light of the full moon (which was really just the streetlight outside). I heard jungle creatures. I felt the sticky wetness of the rainforest. Then I got super depressed. Must have been part of the magic of the DMT, because I thought... *What am I doing with my life?*

After everything I'd learned living life in the van at 70 mph, I had regressed back to lifestyle servitude, doing the same thing I'd been doing before: work that didn't really excite me for the sake of making money and paying bills. Hadn't I learned anything?

Later, I took a couple more hits from the DMT pen to try to get some answers and blasted off into outer space. I shot like a rocket past stars and galaxies. I wondered, *Where am I going? To Destination Freedom? I thought I had already arrived. What happened?*

* * *

The next morning, that lost feeling hadn't left me. What was I doing with my life? Where was I headed? Certainly not to Destination Freedom. I was used to having extreme clarity about the life I want to create, but for some reason, my inner compass was pointing in all sorts of directions. Money! Business! Coffee! CBD!

I learned a ton and had a lot of fun living in Denver. But where was that road taking me? Back to "Business Basin," where work and money and bills awaited me. That wasn't where my heart wanted to go — I'd already learned that the hard way. The whole reason I'd built the van and left Austin had been to get away from that.

I was on the wrong road. And I needed to turn around.

I went for a walk in the snow to try to clear my heart and mind. I had grown to love the cold and how alive it made me feel. My shoes produced crunching noises as I made my way through the snow-covered lawn along the river.

I thought about the fact that I'd wanted to be a filmmaker since childhood. That had been my anthem for most of my life. I mean, technically, I already *was* a filmmaker. I had directed a documentary that premiered at the Illuminate Film Festival. And entrepreneurs paid me good money to make promotional films about events, businesses, and products. But I wanted to write scripts and direct actors in big-budget blockbusters that would play to millions in theaters all over the country.

Every kid has a dream like mine. Sometimes it's to be a fireman. Other times, it's to be an astronaut or a racecar driver. But discovering these destinations isn't always that easy. And for some reason, it's even harder to stay on track with those dreams.

Once I got to film school, I found that many of my peers were just in it for fun or for money or because the idea of Hollywood had been glamorized. When they discovered how much work it took to make films, many of them quit. Even more jumped ship after film school when they realized how tough the film industry really is: sixteen-hour days, politics, nepotism, low wages for many years, and living in a super-expensive city while starting out by getting people coffee. It's an industry that tests your resolve. But for me, it was a no-brainer. I enjoyed making films so much that I knew that I'd be doing it for the rest of my life, regardless of how hard it was.

> Follow your bliss.
>
> —*Joseph Campbell*

I had forgotten that the van was about living in alignment. I had forgotten that the van was about living my dreams NOW instead of "someday." It was time to take myself seriously, which meant putting my dreams first, taking responsibility for my own life (because I am the driver), asking my heart (my compass) what it wanted, pointing my steering wheel in that direction (with my decisions and choices), and putting my foot on the gas (putting it into action)!

How can you get to your destination if you don't even know where you're going?

If your compass/GPS is your heart, your destinations are your most heartfelt desires. So, what does your heart want most? And what do those destinations look like? Be as specific as possible. Clarity is key. Trust that your heart knows what is best. It is a very intelligent organ.

We actually do a lot of thinking with our hearts. The heart creates more electricity than the brain, so in many circumstances, we think and react with our hearts quicker than we can consciously process with our brains. We are literally feeling around blind corners with our hearts.

What is it that your heart desires most? Your emotions are a helpful guidance system for helping to clarify your destination. How do you know? Because it feels good, and it feels right. What makes you feel blissful? That's your destination.

Why waste a single moment doing something that you don't enjoy? There are always challenges, failures, unfulfilled expectations, fears, and mistakes — these things don't feel good. But your destination should raise your emotional state so much that it makes the tough stuff inconsequential.

Not long after this life-changing realization, my phone rang. An old client wanted me to pitch him a proposal for a big project! I immediately began to think up as many excuses as I could to say NO, but then he explained the project.

He needed some new external-facing content to teach students how to save money. It would require that I travel to interview financial experts all over the country. He wanted it to have creative and engaging stories about people saving money. He wanted me to make the budget as big as possible, so I'd have no limitations. And he wanted me to have complete creative freedom. I would be in charge. The vibe was: Just take the idea and run with it!

Hmm, I thought. *Interesting.*

What a cool combination: money and storytelling. After my own relationship to money had changed as a result of living in the van, money was a subject I was interested in learning more about, and I loved the idea of using my filmmaking skills to explore that.

I had literally just stated to the universe that I wanted to be a full-time filmmaker. And somehow, I'd stumbled upon a major film project. It wasn't the project of my dreams, but at least it was headed in the right direction. A simple documentary with subject matter that personally interested me, and I would have the creative freedom to do whatever I wanted. Plus, a client who was actually willing to pay for all my travels. I'll take it!

I went to a coffee shop to type up a proposal immediately. Then I left Denver for Washington. I had plans to leave Janüs the van at my dad's place while I did some international travel…

> If you don't know where you are going, any road will get you there.
>
> —*Lewis Carroll*

DETOUR #3

Marfa, TX

And now for another detour from my story. A detour to one of my favorite destinations on the road…

After hours of driving through nothing but empty desert and ranch land, I finally arrived at a Prada store. Yes, a Prada store, in the middle of nowhere, filled with Prada merchandise… and dead bugs.

This Prada store is a special one. You can't open the door, you can't talk to a store clerk, and you can't shop there because… it's an art installation.

Welcome to Marfa, Texas — an entire city of art in the middle of nowhere, surrounded by miles of natural desert. This makes for some bizarre and beautiful photography. Fortunately, I was prepared. I knew that I couldn't make an epic cross-country trip like this without a good camera.

I have a special kinship with cameras. I even have VHS footage of the first time I touched a camera, when I was about a year old. It was Christmas, I was wearing a tuxedo, and my mom just happened to be operating the VHS camcorder the moment my dad handed me his Nikon F2.

Something magical happens when there's a camera in my hand. I don't understand why, but my brain works differently when I'm holding a camera. Everything else fades away. I see everything differently. I feel good… I'm truly happy. I even went through a period in film school when I kept a camera on me 24/7. I was obsessed.

I think my obsession stems from how gratifying it is to be able to capture something I see in the moment. In this way, photography is unlike other art mediums. It allows me to express myself in a more immediate way. It really does become addicting.

I didn't really have the money to buy a new camera for my vanlife adventure thanks to the fact that all my money was going toward travel necessities, so I bought a Canon 6D with a credit card. For the record, I do not suggest this financing method unless you can pay it off in a month, but I had a special need to be able to document my journeys.

New camera in hand, I was ready for this unique art installation filled with expensive merchandise, totally inaccessible to the public, in the middle of nowhere, for nobody to see. Maybe it's meant to be a comment on how silly and insignificant vanity merchandise really is. There must be tens of thousands of dollars of merchandise inside. How it hasn't been robbed yet, I don't know. (I thought about it myself, for a split second, but Prada's not my style.)

Usually, the gentrification of a community occurs due to the influence of real estate developers and entrepreneurs. But Marfa is a city of cowboys, with a population of about a thousand, gentrified by artists, resulting in something akin to an art amusement park.

Marfa first caught the eye of minimalist installationist Donald Judd in the 1970s, who moved to the tiny western town from New York to get away from the city life that had grown hollow and boring for him. He bought an old army base to act as the location for his permanent installations — over 100 total, located in and around old army barracks and structures. Since then, his foundation, Chinati, has purchased several other buildings in Marfa to preserve the buildings and to house his work.

Because of Judd's presence, other artists and galleries slowly migrated to Marfa, making it a hub for obscure contemporary art of all kinds. And as a result, the city has become a surreal juxtaposition of dilapidated buildings from the Old West right next door to brand new hotels, four-star restaurants, and revamped 1880s buildings housing rare and expensive collections from major gallery owners.

During my visit to Marfa, I saw a young couple walking out of an unmarked building downtown. There were no signs or displays of any kind on the exterior, which made me curious. I wanted to know what was inside, so I decided to investigate.

I opened the door and found myself in a large empty conference room. A nice lady was sitting at a table near the door. She was the owner of the building. Along the walls, I saw shapes and colors, and when I got closer, I realized that they were giant canvases — screen prints. They looked very familiar, and upon further research, I learned that they were Andy Warhol's *Last Supper* works — three of them, valued at about $8 million each.

Right in front of me, in the middle of nowhere, was $24 million worth of art, inside an unmarked building, next-door to a dilapidated gas station, next-door to a four-star restaurant, across the street from more abandoned buildings surrounding a brand new modern hotel, with an actual cowboy riding his horse down the street.

The juxtaposition was bizarre. It was a photographer's wet dream. Everywhere you looked, 360 degrees, was a cover image. I couldn't put my camera down. Later, I followed some "Gallery Open" signs to what was actually a Dutch lady's house that had been converted into a gallery. As I admired the fascinating art from all over the world, the Dutch lady — who still lived there — was feeding a dozen stray cats in and around the house.

Art can be *anything*. It can be any medium. It can be material or immaterial. It can be your words, your actions, or your lifestyle. And, as I learned in Marfa, art can even be an entire city. I highly recommend a trip to Marfa. It might just inspire you to be more creative.

By the time I left, I had a bunch of photographs of Marfa that I was super excited to edit. And something interesting happened with my photography. Having a camera on me all the time totally turned me on. I was electrified by rediscovering something that I love to do. My energy changed, my mood changed, and I became a different person.

Plus, my skills sharpened. Eventually, I was recognized for my vanlife photography and booked a photo gig shooting a corporate event for one of my dad's clients — that one gig alone paid for the price of the camera.

Chapter 31:

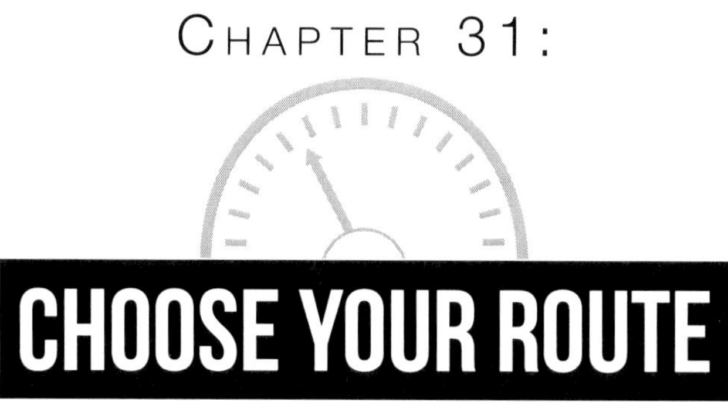

CHOOSE YOUR ROUTE

Bend, OR — June 2019

After a hiatus from the vanlife — living in Denver, followed by a trip to Hawaii, and finally Peru — I craved the road once again.

Eventually, I heard back from the client who had reached out to me about the big project that would combine money and storytelling. I learned that my proposal had not only been accepted but was also highly anticipated. They had never done anything like a film series before.

The plan was for seven episodes, each seven to fifteen minutes long, which would add up to just about ninety minutes of material — the equivalent of a feature film. It would be a major undertaking and would involve interviewing a dozen subjects all over the country, from San Francisco to Texas to Washington DC and Florida, hiring several crew members, and doing several months of editing, color grading, motion graphics, sound work, and music.

So the van adventure wasn't over yet! And I still had so much of the country I wanted to see.

The one corner of the US that Janüs and I hadn't visited yet was New England. And I knew it would be the hardest trip thus far, not only because it was the farthest away from my unofficial home base, but also because I wasn't as familiar with the area and only knew a few people there. But I was gonna get there if it was the last thing I did. Fortunately, all expenses would be paid by the client this time, which would also help me pay off my debt, so one less thing to worry about.

I left Washington in the rearview mirror. Onward to New England!

* * *

Now that I knew my destination, all I had to do was figure out how to get there. But I only had a vague idea of where I wanted to go: over there — that way!

I knew where my GPS (my heart) was telling me to go. I was going to take the van to shoot this film in New England. I also knew my fuel source (my why). My goal was to transition into being a full-time filmmaker.

I had the gas money: a client willing to pay for my travel expenses. So I prepared by making a basic itinerary for the interviews I needed to film in New England. Nevertheless, I knew the details would have to be decided in the moment. All I needed was to map the route.

I knew my first stop on the eight-week road trip to New England would be down to San Diego to have my mom fix some things in the van and make a new cushion for the couch. I've been making the drive from Port Townsend to So Cal since I was a kid, and there are many ways to get there and back. You can take the scenic route on Highway-1 through Big Sur — much slower and more dangerous, but absolutely beautiful. You can take the 101 through the Bay Area — a little bit faster and still visually stimulating. Or you can take the I-5 through Sacramento — the fastest option, but a boring and non-scenic straight shot through farmland.

I had made the drive so many times that I had seen it all. I wanted to do something different this time, so instead of going through Grants Pass in Oregon, I decided to take the 97 to hit the towns of Bend, Deschutes, Sunriver, Crater Lake, Weed, and Mt. Shasta.

We used to have our family reunions at Sunriver, so I had been to Bend before, but not since I was a kid. It's a really nice place, and I like it.

I wanted to relax, so I went to a local marijuana dispensary — a tiny mom-and-pop shop in the living room of a house in a residential area. I got a joint with the citrus terpene profile that works best with my personal endocannabinoid system and talked to the owner of the shop for a bit.

"I'm new to town. Where should I go?" I asked.

"To the caves," he said.

My eyes lit up. Apparently, spelunking is a popular pastime in Bend because of all the ancient volcanic activity, which has carved out all sorts of caves of wonders! I had to check it out.

After a puff, I didn't have a lot of time to get food before the nightly movie started. So I went to the closest restaurant, which was next door to the theater. It happened to be a Peruvian restaurant named Hola! The host was very nice and wore makeup — his hands were soft and delicate. The bartender was also very nice and particularly well-groomed, and I again noted his soft hands. They hovered uncomfortably close to my face, wearing big smiles as I ordered. I'm not sure if they were gay or just very friendly, but it was an interesting way to greet a new customer. I ordered some simple fish, rice, and potatoes.

While I waited for my food, the bartender gave me a free taste of a drink made from raw prickly pear, and *wow*! I ate my food in the van and was delighted to find that it was way better than I'd expected. The potatoes came in a purple cylinder-shaped cake, and the ahi tuna was perfectly cooked. Then I smoked the rest of my joint and headed into the theater.

I camped under the stars in the lovely Deschutes National Forest (where boondocking is permitted), and the next morning, I drove East on the 18 ("China Hat Road") to go spelunking. Right outside Bend there are several caves, including Skeleton Cave, Arnold Ice Cave, and Hidden Forest Cave, which is exactly what it sounds like: a cave hidden in a giant crater-like impression that has its own hidden forest. From inside the cave, it looks like a secret fairy grotto. It's the bee's knees.

So, why do I share all these details with you? Because this is a trip I had made literally dozens of times before. And yet, because I took the path less traveled, it became a totally unique experience.

I easily could have taken the faster route on the I-5 or the scenic route through the redwood forest like I usually do, but I wanted an adventure. And an adventure is what I got.

This is exactly the kind of route I want to take through life.

Once you know your destination(s), the next question is... how do you want to get there?

Despite what some people might lead you to believe, there are multiple ways of getting anywhere. Should you take the slower scenic route or the freeway to get there ASAP? What stops do you want to make along the way? Do you want to take surface streets to see the city and avoid traffic? Or take the highway and risk heavy traffic? Sometimes I purposely avoid major freeways — too many people trying to go my way, so the barrier to entry is too high. I don't care that it'll take me longer to take surface streets through suburbia, because I'd much rather drive 30 mph with nobody in front of me than 40 mph stuck in traffic.

When applying this principle to your life, ask yourself, "Is there a way for me to combine my destinations?" If you want a family *and* a successful career, how can you make sure you reach both destinations? One possibility is to hit your career hard first, and once you get to a certain level, take your foot off the gas, slow down a little, and start a family. Or you can start a family first so you can build a good support system around you that will push you toward your goals. It's up to you.

How do you want to get there?

* * *

After Bend, I mountain biked down Mt. Bachelor with my buddy Steve, explored Sunriver, gawked at the awe-inspiring Crater Lake, shopped in Weed where I bought a magnet for the van that says "I Love Weed!," and meditated at the majestic Mt. Shasta. I often crisscross the country like this to make sure I hit all the places I want to see. On the New England trip, for example, I'd decided to go down to So Cal first to see my mom, then up through Colorado to visit a friend. I then made my way over to Michigan and Wisconsin to do some sightseeing where my dad grew up, and continued through upstate New York, where I would finally veer south and work my way down the East Coast through New England. It may seem like a roundabout route, but the path to success never looks straight.

> What's your road, man? — holyboy road, madman road, rainbow road, guppy road, any road. It's an anywhere road for anybody anyhow. Where body how?
>
> *Jack Kerouac, On the Road (1957)*

CHAPTER 32:

TRANSMISSION = TRANSITIONS

Decorah, IA — July 2019

I had been through the Pacific Northwest a handful of times, So Cal several times, Texas and Colorado a few times, and Florida twice. But never the Northeast. It was the only place Janüs hadn't visited yet. My mind was excited, but my body was not.

I stayed in San Diego with my mom for a bit, getting some upgrades for Janüs's interior, followed by Colorado for a week. While driving through the Rockies, I started to feel strange.

I was kind of tired and depressed, kind of confused, and kind of lost. This struck me as odd, considering that the journey was just beginning, so I hadn't been on the road very long. Maybe it was the altitude again. Maybe it was the prospect of living in the van again for another couple of months. Or maybe I'd drunk too much coffee that morning or too many margaritas the night before. It could have been any combination of things. But as I made my way across Nebraska, it only got worse. I was starting to have full-blown anxiety attacks. What the heck was going on?!

I was on my way to Decorah, Iowa, where a good friend had started his new chiropractic business. I was supposed to arrive on Monday, but I called him in emergency mode to ask if I could come a day early because I was freaking out.

"Luckily, one of us on this phone call is experienced with helping anxiety," he said, "so come on over. Take your time. We've got sausage and corn on the grill, and we'll take care of you."

Thank goodness. What a great friend.

Apparently, Decorah is settled inside of a massive, four-mile crater made from a meteorite which is thought to have crashed down over 470 million years ago. It is said to be a very grounding place, much different than what you'd expect from the rest of Iowa. In fact, this town with a population of only 7,700 has its own farmers market, a co-op (of which half the town are members), an art school, the second-best brewery in the world (it won the award for "Best Beer in the World" a few years back), and more five-star farm-to-table restaurants and yoga places than any other city in Iowa. Plus, it's littered with conscious entrepreneurs of all types. It's like the energy inside the crater has created its own little world.

As I descended into the valley of the crater, the air became cool and calm, the energy started to settle, and I began to see little glowing lights everywhere. The cornfields were littered with fireflies that would glow as I passed by. There were so many of them that they would hit my windshield and explode, and the chemicals contained therein would chemically bond and continue to glow. My entire windshield glowed bright green. It was out of this world. I arrived just in time for a drink and a chat with my buddy before going to sleep.

* * *

The next morning, I woke up, did my morning routine, lifted some weights, went for a run, and felt amazing. After a cold shower and coffee enema, I felt even more amazing. Then I made the cleanest, purest, most delicious green protein shake.

And, all at once, my anxiety came back full-force.

I was starting to notice a pattern. It was like every time I ate something, my anxiety would take hold of me, so I just refrained from eating for a while.

After my host came home from work, he saw how stressed I was. Just by looking at me, he could see that my spine was out of alignment at the base of my skull, which is the vertebra that protects the nerves of the sympathetic and parasympathetic nervous systems. He said that because of this pressure, I was essentially in fight or flight mode all the time, which turns off the digestive system to better enable the body to fight or flee (this is why a deer poops right before running away from a predator). His theory was that this was why I'd been experiencing crazy anxiety every time I ate.

"Let's go to the office and get you an X-ray," he said.

The X-ray revealed that my head was tilting to one side, and the top vertebra was tilted forward about 7 degrees (that's a lot), resulting in a ton of inflammation. Just as he'd expected, this was putting pressure on the nerves that tapped right into the parasympathetic nervous system.

He put me down on the table and did some quick tests with my legs and arms. As soon as he touched me, he felt my anxiety. "Wow, you got it bad."

He made just three quick adjustments to my neck, which popped hard and loud. The adjustment hurt so much that I saw a bright white light. I immediately felt a huge flood of bliss come up from my toes to the top of my skull. All at once, I felt super emotional. First, I started laughing out loud uncontrollably. Then I started crying. All the while, he kept his hands on my head and neck to help mold the cartilage and muscles back to where they were supposed to be.

I thanked him profusely as I got up.

"Take it slow for a bit," he said.

I could barely walk. I felt dizzy and disoriented. Then he put me in a zero gravity chair and sat in the chair next to me so we could talk. We talked about the effects of my chosen lifestyle on my body. The fact that I spent my days staring down at a computer or a phone screen all day long, driving all day long, living in a hectic, go-go-go environment fueled by lots of coffee... This perfect storm would naturally cause problems in my gut.

Because my head was pointed down literally all day long, it was pushing the C1 (atlas) vertebrae down, placing pressure on the nerves that controlled the gut and essentially turned off the signals to my digestive system, which causes indigestion, celiac disease, autoimmune disorders, etc. His explanation resonated with me deeply, and I could tell what he was doing by educating me: My understanding of the situation was part of my healing. This guy was not just any chiropractor but a very powerful healer.

It was looking like the van lifestyle was no longer healthy for me. My body was already telling me to slow down. But I still had 3,500 miles to go to New England, Florida, and then Austin. Maybe it would behoove me to stop traveling so much, settle down in one place, stop drinking coffee/caffeine, do more yoga, and be gentler with myself to allow myself to relax and get grounded.

I could see the beginning of the end of the van journey.

* * *

Afterward, we went out to a nice farm-to-table restaurant for a fancy dinner. It was delicious, but it also revealed my eating habits.

"Dude, slow down," my friend said. He actually got upset with me.

The way I eat is a little embarrassing. I eat like I haven't eaten in days. Ravenous. Like a wolf. And, also like a wolf, I eat a lot.

I appreciated him checking me on this. I had been going, going, going, and the anxiety was my body's way of telling me, "SLOW DOWN." I pride myself on being fast at everything (driving, learning, excelling, doing the dishes, running, even grocery shopping). Generally, I do most things twice as fast as the average human being. I just can't help it. I move through the world quickly, and I don't like waiting.

My chiropractor friend helped me to focus on chewing more slowly and changing my relationship with food. I still struggle with it to this day, but honestly… it was the best meal I've ever had. Not just because of the farm-to-table ingredients and incredible chef, but because I was actually able to enjoy it. The taste of the food in my mouth was overwhelming. The duck was so juicy and rich — a little saltiness perfectly paired with the sweetness of the local red wine that came from vineyards right down the road. I was overdosing on endorphins. Time froze, and I was stuck in the moment.

The feeling was actually a little overwhelming, and my anxiety came back for a second. I breathed into the bite of food in my mouth, and the high was so overpowering that I had to close my eyes, shutting down my other senses. Imagine how your gut would digest this well-chewed food as opposed to wolfing it down. Imagine how you'd digest an experience...

Interesting things happen when you choose to slow down. Your awareness expands, and you're able to really experience things and get more from each moment.

It's important to know when to shift gears. To know how long you can be in high gear and when to put it in park. How do you know when it's the right time to slow down? Self-knowledge. This requires knowing yourself intimately, understanding your limits, and recognizing what signals your body sends you when it needs to slow down.

Trust your body. It is very wise. It knows what it needs.

This is your transmission. So how do you shift gears? Some people need alcohol, coffee, or marijuana. Some people need Netflix. Some people just need a hot bath or a visit to the gym — or fourteen hours of sleep. What works for you? What allows you to transition smoothly from go-go-go to relaxation — from your old home to a new job, from a broken leg back to your workout routine? You can't just go, go, go all the time. For your own good, you've got to know how to shift gears.

The way I shift gears is by doing *nothing*. To transition from a heavy stint of travel to focused work time, all I need is a place I can stay for a day or two to relax and veg out, have a coffee enema, jerk off, watch some movies, smoke some weed, cook a delicious meal, hang out in a jacuzzi, or take a hot bath — just do some relaxing stuff with no work involved. Then I can get back into my routine and get back to work.

The next day, we floated the river for four hours. It was so relaxing, and the fresh Iowa waters washed away the rest of my anxiety. Then I was ready to get back on the road.

Chapter 33:

VANXIETY

Hiawatha, MI — July 2019

So many green trees. I hardly saw anything in Wisconsin but trees. Trees for days and days.

The repetitive trees were hypnotizing. For a while, I thought I might be driving in circles. I could no longer remember how long it had been since I'd started traveling. A few weeks, maybe. How many? Ten? But I had only been driving for about fifteen minutes that morning when I started to get the sickness again. Uh-oh…

Although the loneliness was beginning to negatively affect my mental health, there are some advantages to being alone. Many long hours on the road means a massive amount of quiet, pensive meditation — much more than you usually get in today's busy world. The low-frequency rumble of rubber against asphalt puts your mind into a meditative state. Thinking. Reflecting. Processing. The road gives the subconscious time to churn through all those memories, events, thoughts, pains, failures, and successes. Like an oven, all of these ingredients cook together and give rise to a sort of sour bread. And sometimes, the best breads take the longest to bake.

It'd been a while since I'd had so much downtime alone to myself. Things began to emerge. Demons began to creep up from my subconscious. Fears, pains, traumas, my childhood…

And my anxiety returned. It was a strange feeling of longing for something, but I didn't know what. The same sickness Spanish voyagers would get on long-term expeditions across the Atlantic — the same issues experienced by explorers crossing the Antarctic and astronauts on long-term space missions. It feels like a sort of spiritual sickness. Like a mix of loneliness, depression, homesickness, confusion, and a hangover. If not treated, it will eventually become a disease, affecting your physical health.

My consciousness shrank and curled up like a snail, back inside my head where it's safe and warm. My vision narrowed. All my senses were muted. It was like I was watching everything through a television screen. All that was left was an acute awareness of the following: *I am dying, everything is bad, nothing will help me, the world is ending.* It usually lasted for a few hours, and almost nothing helped. The worst part was that when you're that ill, your instincts tell you to quarantine, even though connection is what you need most in the moment.

I started to get dizzy. I had to stop, so I pulled over to a rest area. I could barely walk, and the slightest movement made the dizziness worse. All I could do was lie down on the floor of the van. My body and mind just needed to be still for a second.

I was parked underneath a wind turbine, and for some reason, the spin of its blades helped counteract the spinning world around me. So I just stared at the wind turbine as its blades slowly rotated, around and around, around and around.

Finally, I called my buddy Steve, my best friend from third grade, who had followed in my footsteps and started building his own van. I had inspired him, he said, to start by building out the back of his pickup so he could sleep and eat at work since he worked the night shift. The experience had worked out so well for him that he'd bought a Sprinter and started building it out, too. After finishing his build, he and his fiancée set out on an epic van adventure across the US in their Sprinter, which they dubbed Claude Van-Damme. They had an epic blast, and we met up several times to forage for morel mushrooms in Oregon, bike down Mt. Bachelor, and hike the Olympic Mountains with bears.

Even though I was currently having some challenges with the vanlife, I was elated to hear that my chosen lifestyle was having a positive impact on those around me. In fact, he wasn't the only friend I knew who had started a van adventure after seeing me do it. (They may not have done it directly because of me, but I like to think so.)

* * *

After half an hour of chatting with Steve, my anxiety was gone. On the outside, it may have appeared that I was broken down on the side of the road, too dizzy to move, but inside, I was glowing with a bright smile. Finally, I was able to get back in the cockpit, took a deep breath, have a few words with myself, spark the engine, and continue driving.

But alas, my old friend, anxiety, returned.

Damn it! Why did this keep happening to me?

I didn't know what else to do. So this time, instead of trying to get rid of it through breathing, stretching, smoking, meditating, talking to a friend, or sleeping… I embraced it. I leaned into it. I needed to let this energy out, so I began singing.

"My friend 'vanxiety'!
So much piety!
I'm here for you.
Let me make it clear to you.
Anything you need,
take anything you see."

That's right. I sang an ode to my friend, "vanxiety." And suddenly, I got a strange sense of déjà vu.

When I talked to my anxiety, I heard it talking back. And it sounded so familiar. The lonely anxiety I was feeling on the road was a sensation I had felt before. But not recently. It was from some other place, at some other time. Years ago. Why was this feeling so familiar?

I searched back through my life. Way, way back. And I saw a blonde little Nicky with bright blue eyes, maybe five or six years old.

Memories of my childhood began to flood my conscious mind: the baby bird I found that had fallen from its nest outside the pool at my mom's apartment complex. The day I stepped on a hornet while walking barefoot through the grass and my toe ballooned like a tomato. The dark, scary house my mom lived in with one of her boyfriends who smelled like cigarettes. The time I thought I needed to fart but accidentally pooped my pants, but nobody was home to help me. The big boarding house my dad lived in with almost no furniture. The macadamia nut trees in the backyard — I could taste them in my mouth, hear the sounds of the pigeons cooing in the morning.

Then my memory took me to fifth grade, when I decided to attend a different middle school than my girlfriend. She kissed me on the cheek while we were walking home on the last day of fifth grade, and I told my dad I didn't want to go to her middle school because all my friends were going to Bernardo Heights. I remember gripping the back of the smooth white leather couch because I knew it was a lie. All those lunch periods in high school, spent alone in the library because I didn't want to socialize with my peers. All those parties in college I avoided because I had a legitimate social phobia. All these memories crept up uninvited, as if my mind's eye was searching through old records that matched the same emotion I was feeling in the van. Then I ran out of records.

Like a movie reel running out to an empty spool, the memories ended, and my focus came back to the road in front of me. I realized that this lonely feeling I had on the road had been with me through my entire youth — I just hadn't felt it in a long time.

Back then, being constantly shuttled between two single parents, I was often sleeping on the couch, in their bed, or on a cot in the corner, until I shared a room with my sister before she went off to college. I felt more like a piece of furniture that they had to move. And that, I now realized, may have developed into an unhealthy habit of socially isolating myself from my peers throughout my entire school career.

The gears inside a combination lock aligned, and CLICK! The doors of perception opened.

No wonder I had decided to live the life of a lone wolf in a van. It made complete sense that staying in one spot with the same people would feel unnatural to me.

Moving around with no community is all I ever knew until high school. So *of course* I don't know how to create "HOME." Of course I don't know how to ground myself and grow roots. Of course I don't know how to find my community and maintain long-term relationships. Of course I don't know how to build a family. Because, for as long as I could remember, I'd never had any of that.

Moving around all the time, constantly creating new relationships, was my default setting. The van was simply a way to continue carrying out the programming I had learned as a child. Perhaps growing roots even frightened me to some extent. Maybe I even equated it to being trapped. Being stuck in the same place — in the same house, with the same people — scares the shit out of me. No breathing room. Claustrophobia. It feels like chains to me.

Despite how uncomfortable I felt, it all at once became clear to me. *Connection*. This was obviously what I needed for my own mental health and wellness. I could have paid for years of personal therapy to figure this out, but for some reason, it was a van that did it for me.

Thanks, Janüs.

That was when I noticed that I was driving past a large body of water. So I pulled over. For a second, I thought I was back in Florida with its white-sand beaches and turquoise water, but it was Lake Superior. I'd had no idea it was so beautiful. The beach was sandy, and the water was serene. The tranquility of the lake mirrored my newfound inner peace.

Wading through the beautiful water, I realized that my anxiety had disappeared.

Something had shifted in me. All those struggles I had battling loneliness, all that time spent with no human connection, all the pain I felt burning in the hell of social isolation — my friend "vanxiety" was simply trying to tell me something.

Well, I finally got the message. And I decided I would isolate myself no more.

When I considered my isolated childhood, I knew I needed deeper and more fulfilling human connection. I needed to be around my loved ones more. I needed to learn how to deepen my connections with my friends and not just run away in a van when things got tough.

To jumpstart this habit, I made sure I had friends to stay with along the rest of the trip through New England. This meant that I needed to switch up my itinerary and roadmap a bit.

This was more than a road trip. Janüs was changing me from the inside-out in ways I had never anticipated.

Chapter 34:

CARPOOL

Wappinger Falls, NY — August 2019

After Janüs and I ascended the windy roads into the magnificent hills of Wappinger Falls, NY, I arrived at the property. There was a line of cars backed up for a mile or so. Everybody was being turned away by hired security. They told me there was no more parking available on the property, so I had to park down at the train station, and a shuttle would come and pick me up.

It was so humid that I was sweating as I changed my clothes. A shuttle finally came by to pick up a few stragglers, myself included. I hoped I didn't smell. The driver of the shuttle was an artist, like many of the passengers. Very cool people. Very friendly. I felt accepted already.

Once past the gates of the property, we drove through what seemed like an endless forest. There was some interesting art along the road every once in a while, including a giant hand made of twigs and branches standing in the loving hand mudra.

The shuttle dropped us off in a cul-de-sac driveway. The Victorian mansion was packed. For a second, I got a little nervous. There were a lot more people than I thought there'd be... *too* many. But I had decided to connect more during my travels through New England, so I pushed myself out of my comfort zone and stepped inside.

This was just one of many full moon gathering celebrations at Alex Grey's COSM (Chapel of Sacred Mirrors).

I had been following the visual artist Alex Grey ever since stumbling on an open gallery showing of his "Sacred Mirrors" in Southern California back in film school. I had never seen art like his before, but it was as if it had always existed. The way he sees the world is all-encompassing, visually representing all the systems of energy and matter. With the anatomical accuracy of a modern Da Vinci, he shows humans as the electric, magnetic, energetic, magical, multi-dimensional conscious beings that we are.

Grey is one of my favorite contemporary artists living and working today. His work will undoubtedly go down in art history as some of the most important of this century — if not for its quality and style, then certainly for its ability to define the consciousness shift we're experiencing as a species during these times. His art is a lighthouse for all those lost new-agers trying to relive the 1960s. And through the COSM community project, the Greys have become the epicenter for the conscious community in the New England area. So when I learned that he and his wife Allyson had opened a community center, I had to check it out.

The formal part of the gathering was fun and delivered what you'd expect from a conscious community: meditation, music, speakers on esoteric topics, art presentations, etc. Alex and Allyson led the ceremony together as we celebrated the full moon. Seeing them work together was sweet and inspiring.

Then came a big party! And that was super fun because everybody was so open and friendly. It was fun just to people-watch. Especially some of the young yogi girls with their conscious fashion and dreadlocks. No need for bras or razors!

Hordes of people admired some of Alex's most recent artworks on the walls, and a long line at the Mushroom Cafe wrapped around the hallways, serving mushroom tea and vegan treats while a rave was happening in the next room. I could hear the bump of the heavy bass through the walls. I stepped inside for a second, but there were too many drugs in there for me.

A performance of fire twirlers drew me back outside. Then somebody started a massive bonfire, so I gravitated toward that. Soon it started raining, and everybody ran inside while I basked in the warm glow of the fire. That was when I met the fire keeper, an interesting character dressed in traditional Chinese silks, including a cone-shaped coolie hat and kilt-like robes. For the record, he was definitely not Chinese — white, as far as I could tell. His job for the night was to tend the fire.

Since we were the only two left at the bonfire, we struck up a conversation in the rain. He was a very friendly guy, and I soon learned that he had another job. Apparently, he was the head builder for the Chapel of Sacred Mirrors project, which at the time was just a half-finished building a few hundred yards behind us. The structure was on its way to becoming a sacred chapel unlike anything ever seen before, dedicated to worshipping art and nondenominational unity. It's intended to be the final resting place for Alex Grey's most revered Sacred Mirrors, the paintings I saw back in film school.

The fire keeper and I spoke mostly about women and marriage. He had just had a kid and was loving being a dad. But balancing family with work presented some challenges. We both agreed on how important family was, including connecting with loved ones. I understood this truth all too well. He didn't know it, but our conversation was exactly the intimacy I needed. It was very healing. It looked like my decision to connect more was already paying off.

Overall, I was discovering that being alone in the van isn't so bad if I could be around like-minded people every once in a while. I realize now that it was the community events that really fueled me up while on the road. Was I actually an extrovert? My whole life, I'd thought I was an introvert, but clearly, the van had changed that. Harmonious connection with other like-minded people makes everything more bearable.

The fire keeper offered me some free food from the pop-up restaurant tent, where a large group of privileged attendees with special bracelets were sipping wine and laughing, but I wasn't really hungry. So I decided to pee in the woods and head to bed. I waited in the rain for a shuttle to take me back down to the van, then drove Janüs back up to the property to park in the woods for the night. I heard celebratory partying continuing late into the night.

* * *

In the morning, I returned and explored the grounds in the daylight to check out all the cool installation art and sculptures. It was a very inspiring place. Then I headed to New York City, where I spent the whole day walking from Central Park to Wall Street on an epic photo adventure. My feet hurt, but I was still on a high from the opportunity to connect with other conscious creative folks like me. I took the subway back to the van and got out of the city before dark.

I was heading south to New Jersey when the fire keeper's words came back to me. He had confided in me how difficult it was to have a newborn child, and he longed for an untethered life like mine in the van. But…

"I'm so blessed," he'd quickly added.

Even though he was experiencing something challenging and maybe even painful as a result of his family relationships, he still felt blessed. How beautiful to feel that duality.

I am often surprised to hear that many of my friends don't even want kids. Perhaps Millennials are too narcissistic to be responsible for other human beings. Or maybe we're just too poor, and the gap in the cost of living is too high to justify having kids nowadays. One common excuse I hear is, "I wouldn't want to bring a child into such an awful world." I don't even know what to do with that one. The world I live in is pretty amazing, and it would be the greatest honor to be able to continue my genealogy.

Because I had never really had a family as a kid, I had always wanted to get married and create a family of my own. In fact, I've wanted a family for as long as I can remember, even when I was a toddler. Longer than I've wanted to be a filmmaker.

"Takes a village," the fire keeper told me.

I guess I'll know when I have a family of my own.

Family consists of the individuals you choose to carpool with. You may not be able to choose your bloodline, but you sure can choose who you carpool with.

Whether it's your team, your spouse, your kids, your friends, or your extended family, carpooling is the commitment to commute with these persons long-term. We're going to the same destination, so let's do it together! The benefits: it's easier/quicker to travel through life with someone else than it is to go alone because you get access to the carpool lane, which is usually less crowded and faster (but not always).

If you want to go fast, go alone. If you want to go far, go together.

African Proverb

I had always focused on being as efficient as possible and moving as fast as I could. The way I see it, I have a lot of ground to cover if I want to go far in life! But reaching my life destinations requires a team. I needed help if I was to be a famous film director, a business owner, a published writer, a land baron, a teacher, a father of two, and a husband. My heart was beginning to open and reveal new destinations that I had always desired but had never considered to be feasible.

I needed a support system. I had gone too long by myself.

I hadn't been expecting any of this. I'd just wanted to make a film in New England and eventually some more films, but it seems that once I turned the steering wheel, there was no stopping. I was already on the road toward my dreams. But now, that road was leading me to *other* destinations I had to stop at first in order to get to my final destination.

In order to make the trip, I needed a new vehicle that could handle the drive. I needed a new engine from "Personal Growth Canyon." I needed a new suspension from "Sharp Town." I needed some new teachers from "Masters Mountain." And I needed some passengers to carpool with.

Like a magical Santa Claus, the road was giving me what I asked for. And family was one of the most important stops on the way — an internal destination to help me along the way to my external destination.

I am so grateful for my grand caravan: the Conederas, Washams, Dials, and Applebys. Who do *you* want to carpool with?

CHAPTER 35:

Philadelphia, PA — August 2019

New Jersey in August was way too hot! I slept on the beach, but it was sticky even without any covers. It was nice to wake up on the beach, and the ocean was a great shower to cool down — but it was still too hot. In the end, I decided to get a hotel in Philly.

I hopped on Priceline and booked a couple of nights in an Extended Stay. But when I arrived in the afternoon, the friendly young African American girl working at the front desk said they were all booked up. She must have been nineteen years old.

"But I have a reservation," I replied.

"Hold on, let me check," she said. She then disappeared into the elevator.

I waited for probably ten minutes before she finally came back to let me know that they had a room for me.

Mmm-kay...

She gave me a keycard, and I proceeded up the elevator and down the dingy hallway. When I got inside the room, it smelled kind of funny. I looked around. Looked fine.

But something didn't feel right.

I threw the blankets off the bed. Nothing. I went into the bathroom. Looked clean enough. I lifted the toilet seat. Fine. But then I saw the bar of hand soap. It had a black hair on it. A black *curly* hair.

I ran back to the bed and put my face in it. It smelled like body odor.

I let out a long sigh of exhaustion. I was so looking forward to just relaxing. But I needed to be a little flexible.

I went back downstairs with my stuff, told the nice young lady at the front desk what I had experienced, and told her I would not be staying there anymore. I wasn't mean about it, just eager to relax. She happily refunded my money. (My guess is that she'd been letting a friend crash in the room or something. A smelly friend.)

* * *

I wasn't about to give up on finding a place to escape the heat, so I went back on Priceline for something a little more expensive. I was trying to keep it cheap because my client was paying for everything, but I found a pretty nice place right in the center of downtown. And it was super cheap. All right, let's do it!

When I got there, it was far beyond what I expected. It was an old bank building that had been converted into a super fancy hotel. When I stepped into the elevator, there were three big black guys sharing a ride with me. I could tell they were athletes.

"Eagles?" I asked them.

"Falcons. We're in town to practice with them."

"Wow! How big is the whole organization when you travel?"

"About a hundred guys. Have a good day, man."

They ducked as they left the elevator.

Cool. Must be expensive to take over a whole hotel like that.

They got off the elevator on the floor with all the meeting and conference rooms. It looked like a party with Gatorade and hors d'oeuvres.

When I got to my room, I was blown away. Super swanky, with a great view of downtown Philly. I took a hot shower immediately, then just laid on the bed, watching movies all night and ordering room service. It had been at least a couple of weeks since the last time I'd stayed anywhere other than the van for the night. I really needed it! How was this only $70 per night? That was just a little more expensive than the smelly Extended Stay! It was as if the universe was saying, "You deserve something nice!"

This would never have happened if I hadn't been willing to be flexible.

* * *

The next morning, I had an amazing American Breakfast at the restaurant downstairs, people-watching the hordes of busy Philadelphians walking by the downtown window. I don't think they could see me watching them, but I could see them. I spotted a young city kid dribbling his basketball as he chatted with his buddies in front of the Ravens' three tour buses. The way the kid moved reminded me of James Dean — could probably be a great actor.

After breakfast, I went for a walk downtown toward the arts district. I got stuck in the City Hall quad with a homeless guy screaming about the caps of plastic bottles, who explained that they reminded him of buttholes and that he doesn't *want* to be reminded of buttholes while he's about to take a drink of water. But the Sprite bottles are okay — their caps are a little wider. I would never have known.

"Only drink Sprite," he said.

Noted.

He kept going on and on about buttholes, but every time I tried to add to the conversation, he cut me off. I was only there to listen, I guess. I asked if I could take a photo of him, but he said no. Just sucking my time from me. So I kept on walking.

In the gardens outside the Rodin Museum, I hung out with a butterfly for several minutes. He just wanted that sweet nectar and didn't mind my presence. So I took some pictures. Then it was on to the Philadelphia Museum of Art, which I visit every time I'm in Philly. It has a wonderful collection. The next day, I shot my interview, spent one more night in Philly, and left for Washington DC.

As always, I enjoyed my stay in Philly immensely. But my journey south was cut short by the weather. Florida was supposed to be my last stop for interviews. From there, I was going to figure out what to do next. But it wasn't meant to be. In fact, I had to cancel my Florida shoots entirely because of hurricane Dorian.

I was bummed because I had already booked an Airbnb in Key West to stay put for a bit and relax. I was hoping to enjoy a writing retreat, visit some of the bars Hemingway frequented, and work on a new screenplay. But by the time I got to shooting my interview in Nashville, all my plans in the south had been canceled. Alabama. Georgia. Florida. Louisiana. All of them.

And just like that, the van adventure was over.

* * *

For the first time in a long time, I had no plans and nowhere to go.

I felt a little uneasy about not knowing what I was going to do. But I took my own advice and decided to be flexible. I changed my plans and decided to head back to Austin. It was an appropriate place to end the van adventure, since that was where it had started.

As important as planning is, it's just as important to stay flexible. Sometimes you find a pube in your plans (sometimes literally), so you gotta roll with the punches. Plans change.

Flexibility allows you to take advantage of unexpected opportunities. Flexibility allows you to bend without breaking when the pressure gets hot. Flexibility also allows you to change or compromise in order to get the most out of life. Lake bamboo, it's your flexibility that makes you strong.

I'm usually very determined and stubborn, but I figured I would need to be flexible in my journey to reach my ultimate destination of being a rich and famous film director with a wonderful wife and kids like I always imagined.

I'm not there yet. It will probably take decades. And it will probably happen in ways I least expect. But I'm on my way.

Chapter 36: Breaking Down

Johnson City, TX — September 2019

I was driving along the 290 through the rolling hills of Texas, my mind wandering, when I smelled something a little off. Suddenly, my dash started screaming at me.

BEEP! BEEP! BEEP!

Red warnings began to flash: *Check Gauges*.

"Which gauges?!" I screamed back. "All of them?"

Smoke began to fill the cab.

Up until this point, in all of the 60,000 miles I had driven in the van, I'd had not one single engine problem. Well, there went Janüs's perfect record.

* * *

My visit with friends in Austin was short but fun. I was planning on heading back to Washington to be with my family for the winter, so I had decided to go on one last adventure before hitting the road the next day.

Exploring the rolling hills of central Texas, I had noticed a castle standing tall and proud along the 290, with signs for "Wine & Views." There are a few wine castles out there off the 290, actually. One is a wine tasting venue, another is a hotel, and a third is an events venue.

I tried to recruit some friends to go wine tasting, but for one reason or another, it hadn't happened. So I decided to check it out on my own. Destination: wine castle!

It was tacky and fun and hot — exactly what you'd expect of a wine castle in the middle of Texas. Lots of middle-aged women. Swords and medieval armor hanging everywhere. Way too much purple.

I tried a few wines and talked to the server about some of the offerings on their list. There were a few I wasn't familiar with. I was surprised to learn that the server was the owner's daughter. The winery was a family-owned business, started by her daddy as a gift to her mother, whose dream had been to start a winery. They had only been open for a few years and were serving European and local Texas wines of their choice, eventually planning to make their own wines after a few years of production. Only a few types of grapes can handle the heat and humidity of Texas — the dark spicy kind. I ordered a glass of my favorite, then sat on the deck to write for a bit. Soon, I was hot and drunk and bored, so I left.

On my way out, a bachelorette party asked me to take a picture of them. Some were very loud, and some were falling over drunk. Fortunately, they had asked the right guy — a pro. I had them first do a professional pic for the family, then a fun one. And they all posed like half-naked strippers.

It was after that, on my way home, when Janüs's radiator blew.

* * *

I pulled over to let the engine cool off. Then I started it back up to see if the problem would persist. Not even a minute later, the temperature gauge was back in the red. I pulled over again and turned off the engine. But this time, I was parked in a very precarious place, on the side of the freeway where there was hardly any shoulder. Just ahead, I saw a saloon. Not a bar. Like, a real saloon, because it's Texas!

Okay, I thought, *I'll pull into the parking lot, call a tow truck, and wait there while I have dinner and some drinks.*

I started Janüs up and managed to get a little farther before the engine overheated again. I pulled over and stopped to cool down.

I waited. Then I sparked it again. This time, I was able to make it to the parking lot before stopping to cool down. Then I started the van back up to park and sit for a while in the shade. I don't think Janüs liked the thick heat and humidity of Texas. Poor guy.

The saloon didn't look like much from the outside, but the sign out front had a picture of a Tasmanian Devil flipping you off.

This'll be interesting.

The interior was a Texas cowboy's fantasy. A huge confederate flag hung behind a disco ball on a karaoke stage. A giant taxidermied longhorn was on the wall. The tables and chairs were hand-made from local wood. Bullets and guns inlaid into the bar and tables. Country music playing on the jukebox. And the sweetest Texas belles serving. But it was a ghost town so far.

I ordered the BBQ and some red wine. It was all right, but that's not the point of saloons, is it? I called a tow and waited for a couple of hours, by myself at first. But slowly, the saloon started filling with cowboys. And one by one, they surrounded me at the bar. Six of them. They all knew each other, too.

Johnson City is a very small town, mostly ranches. It was the hometown of President Lyndon B. Johnson and was named after its founder, his great-uncle. The cowboys had come for ladies' night, but there were no ladies. So it goes.

These guys were mostly retired, but they were the real deal — one ranch owner, one who grew grass for feed, one actual cowboy, a couple of oilers, and one engineer who seemed a bit out of place. And they were all dressed in flannel, cowboy boots, and ten-gallon hats. I was just a silly young city boy to them.

The cowboy sitting next to me was a fellow named Johnny. He seemed to be the leader of the group, the wisest and most respected. We struck up a conversation, and he seemed adamant about teaching this naive city boy what it really meant to be a man. I literally couldn't understand him at first because his rugged country drawl was so thick. We spoke about how city life had changed so much and reminisced about "the way things used to be." We spoke about technology and how nobody seems to be able to actually *do* anything anymore.

And we spoke about practical skills like ranching, camping, fixing cars, hunting, and living off the land.

One of the boys needed some help with his old Chevy pickup, which had been acting up. The engineer said, “No problem, I’ll come over and fix it. How about Tuesday?”

This was and still is the way in so many parts of our country outside of the big cities. People helping each other, sharing their skills for free — as opposed to a mechanic trying to squeeze the maximum amount of money out of you to cover an expensive monthly overhead. I understood this particularly well, considering I had been living in a van for the better part of the last couple of years.

The fact that I was a filmmaker living in a van was pretty intriguing to them. They wanted to know more. Having taught myself some of the practical analog skills that were key to their way of life — construction, auto repair, camping, living at one with nature — my respect for these old cowboys was palpable, and we connected on this level. Even though they clearly had different values and beliefs, particularly their opinions on “that [n-word] president” and the “ignorant people” trying to stop the pipeline. To each their own.

It wasn’t long before Johnny had enough Budweisers in him to open up and share about his past. He got real quiet and leaned in.

“I used to be a Texas oilman. Made good money. One day, a fire broke out. I got burned over fifty percent of my body.” Now that he was closer to me, I could see the scarring on his face, half-covered by his beard. “I’ve experienced more pain than any good Christian should. It was like burning alive in the pits o’ hell. But I just kept asking for one more hour. Just give me one more hour of life in this wonderful place. For two months, I stayed in the hospital until I was healed enough to walk on my own. And the good Lord kept me alive. I figured there must be a reason He wanted to keep me here.”

“What do you think it was?” I asked him.

“To teach me,” he said. “I don’t have a lady, I don’t got no kids. I used to run around a lot, drinking, having fun, but it didn’t serve me or Him. He showed me where I was headin’ — hell.” Johnny fixed his hat and took another swig. “I’m meant to serve.”

"That's why I make movies," I told him.

I explained to Johnny that my purpose is one of contribution — to elevate the consciousness of humanity through the awesome power of storytelling. Storytelling is an effective way to teach valuable wisdom because it engages people emotionally through fun and entertainment.

"You're all right," he said and patted me on the back. "I ain't worried 'bout ya."

We raised our glasses in a toast. Then my tow truck arrived. I don't normally care about what people think of me, but getting the approval of this cowboy was meaningful to me for some reason. He was like the brother I never had.

* * *

Sometimes we find ourselves in a rut, broken down on the side of the road, cursing at the heavens, "Why hast thou forsaken me?!"

Shit happens. Always has, always will. The question is: What are you going to do about it? Maybe God has a very specific plan for your unexpected breakdown — something he's trying to teach you. Maybe He just enjoys watching you writhe in agony broken down on the side of the road. Or maybe things just happen with no meaning at all and it is what it is... Whatever the cause of the breakdown, it's still up to you to create your experience. You're the driver, remember?

Are you going to sit on the side of the road to wine and cry? Are you going to relax and take advantage of the opportunity to not drive for a bit? Or are you going to see it as an opportunity to learn and grow?

I can't imagine what it was like for Johnny to be literally cooked in an oil fire. Johnny chose to see his breakdown as an opportunity to change his ways and serve God. So what was the purpose of my breakdown?

Well, I found it ironic that the van decided to poop out the day before I was planning to leave Austin. I guess I was meant to stay there a little longer.

I had the tow truck drop the van off at the local mechanic that I used while I was living in Austin. Then I made my way back to my friends' house, where I had been staying. They let me stay an extra week until the van was fixed — THANK YOU! Gotta love dependable friends.

I took a day to do some journaling and figure out what I wanted to do with this breakdown. Because something was bothering me — an itch that I couldn't scratch. I soon realized that Janüs and I were on the same page. I wasn't ready to leave either.

I had been traveling so much for so long, and I just wasn't ready to start traveling again. I still needed more grounding, and I wanted more time with my friends. In the end, I decided to stay in Austin for a couple of months, finish this client work, and take some time to write a script. The breakdown ended up being a wonderful gift. But the fact that I no longer felt the desire to be on the road told me that I was nearing the end of the vanlife.

Janüs is very wise. That's why he's my van. Somehow he knew. Maybe he broke down on purpose; he just wanted to stay in Austin for a bit longer. It was where he was born, after all. It was home for both of us. I'm just glad he decided to break down where and when he did, rather than in the middle of nowhere while on my way to Washington. That would have been a nightmare. The AAA lady told me over the phone that the saloon I'd found was just five miles away from being out of their service area. How lucky was that?

Chapter 37:

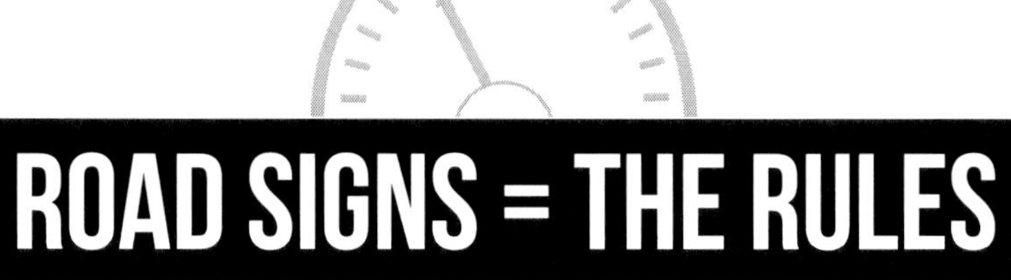

ROAD SIGNS = THE RULES

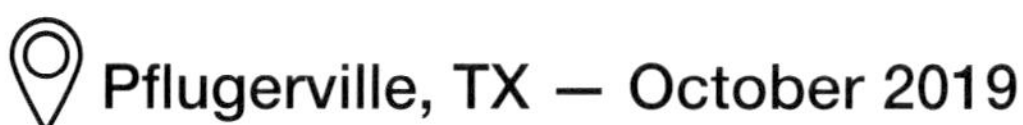

Pflugerville, TX — October 2019

> The three most harmful addictions are heroin, carbohydrates, and a monthly salary.
>
> *Nassim Taleb*

"If you're telling me that you're not going to sleep with me anymore, then I'm going to throw something at you."

Oh, boy… What had I gotten myself into?

After deciding to stay in Austin for a bit longer, I'd needed a place to stay. So I'd decided to crash with a girl I was seeing. What a great idea, I thought! Free shelter, plus a warm body! What's the worst thing that could happen?

Wow. I am an idiot.

I reached out to a couple of my real estate investor friends to see if they happened to have any rooms available in any of their properties and found a room in a tech house in Pflugerville. It was a shithole in a shitty area pretty far outside the city, but it was cheap and I was in a tight spot, so I snatched it up that same day.

My housemates were three nine-to-fivers in the tech industry. One was a programmer from Pakistan working for Apple, another a

Vietnamese programmer working for GM, and the third a white guy in some sort of inventory management at Dell right down the street. This made for an interesting and diverse household. I very much enjoyed it, but it wasn't long before I began to scratch my head at the daily schedule of our little household.

My housemates got up early, went to work between 8 a.m. and 9 a.m., didn't come home until 5 p.m. or 6 p.m., and went straight to their rooms, where they often had to tend to more work. This was kind of nice because I got the whole house to myself all day. They weren't very social and didn't seem to have any friends that I knew of. Neither did they appear to ever hang out with each other. Mostly, they just tended to themselves. From what I could tell, each of them gave his entire week away to a job that they didn't seem to really like. Maybe, deep down, they enjoyed the work or the people, but it didn't seem that way when they got home. And nobody in the house made over $6K/month.

After experiencing the complete freedom of life in my van, my housemates' way of life just seemed ridiculous to me.

Why would anybody ever partake in such a lifestyle? Meanwhile, I only worked a few hours per day, came home at 1 p.m. or 2 p.m. to make myself a big beautiful American breakfast, watched a movie, took a nap, and then worked on my own personal projects that I was doing for fun and personal enjoyment. And I was making about the same amount of money as they were.

My roommates would often come home needing to vent to somebody, and there I was — usually drunk or high, ready to socialize, cooking a delicious dinner that made the house smell wonderful. "Welcome home, honey! Give me a kiss! How was work?" Like a happy, horny housewife. I felt a responsibility to enliven their mundane days. And I heard the most awful stories…

One housemate believed he was being stalked by his manager because of an honest report he had given in his quarterly review. Poor guy! He feared for his life and was stressed all the time. My Pakistani roommate had a good job at Apple and could work from home anytime he wanted, but since he was in the US on a work visa, he was paid as a private contractor and had no benefits. My other housemate had to run an hour a day just to keep his body and mind strong enough to sit at the computer for eight hours a day. His diet consisted of Cheerios, easy-bake pizzas, and animal crackers, and he ran a six-minute mile... *What?!*

These tech guys had “arrived.” They had reached the place you’re supposed to get to — a good job at a reputable company. But they didn’t seem happy at all. In fact, they seemed miserable. Or at least bored. Or maybe they were just exhausted from doing the *same thing* every day. They were stuck in the rat race.

Rat race (noun): a way of life in which people are caught up in a fiercely competitive struggle for wealth or power. An exhausting, usually competitive routine.

I totally empathized with my new housemates, because I had been there before Janüs the van. It was why I felt so compelled to brighten their days. When I’d had my apartment in Austin, all I had focused on was building my business. I got it to six figures four years in a row. Not bad for a starving artist. But it still wasn’t enough. It would never be enough. No matter how much money I made, I always needed more. I reinvested some and saved some, but I mostly spent it on a lifestyle of recurring bills and expenses: phone, internet, nice apartment, car, massage, gym, Netflix, Amazon, Pandora, alcohol, drugs, travel, eating out — all the things I needed to be “happy.” But, as I shared at the start of this book, I was anything *but* happy.

Now I live in a van with no possessions, no bills, hardly any work, hardly any money, but completely free... and happier than I’ve ever been.

Once we started to get to know each other better, my housemates seemed to be enamored with me and my lifestyle.

“You’re a filmmaker? Huh? You travel all the time? What? You have your own business? How? You live in a van? Why? You make your own schedule? You do whatever you want whenever you want? *Whaaaa?*”

My lifestyle seemed so foreign to them. They didn’t know any entrepreneurs. They didn’t know it was even possible because they only knew the one way: the way they had been taught since childhood. On the contrary, I didn’t know anybody who had a job, except my mom. The experience provided valuable perspective for all of us. But whenever I opened my mouth, I projected thoughts and ideas that challenged what they had grown to believe, and it blew their minds.

My housemates helped me realize that the destinations I was trying to reach required me to ignore the road signs, make illegal U-turns, and drive into oncoming traffic. The rules of the road didn't work for me. Never have, never will.

"Film director" is not a normal job. I can't find employment making films; there are no "help wanted" ads with that title, and nobody's going to pay me to do what I love. I have to create my own job by making my own films. I can't follow the street signs like everybody else does because the signs are designed to get you where everybody else is going.

I knew early on that "9-5 Street" wouldn't get me to my desired destination. On my roadmap, that avenue led in the opposite direction, away from where I wanted to go. I had to take alternate routes. I had to do it my way.

Sometimes, you just have to ignore the signs, go the wrong way, and drive into oncoming traffic. But don't worry — people will get out of your way. Because you'll leave them no other choice.

Are you going to follow the signs? Do they lead you to where you want to go?

As this experience wore on, I grew frustrated. The longer I stayed in Austin, the more work I got. And soon, I began to sink back into the production/consumption lifestyle, spending my days doing unfulfilling work to pay bills, because big cities are expensive!

It felt like I was gradually becoming my roommates. I was right back where I'd started when I first decided to build the van. Had I learned nothing on the road? I had to get off at the next exit and reroute.

I decided to head back to Washington to be with my family because I needed their help and support to carpool to Destination Freedom.

By then, it was the end of 2019. I had been living in a van for two years.

Then 2020 happened...

Chapter 38:

THE ARRIVAL

Port Townsend, WA — 2020

Port Townsend was just as dark and gray as I remembered, the drivers just as slow, and the co-op clerks just as crabby. Home sweet home. I was returning anew — this time, not because I had to, but because I wanted to.

I had rediscovered the importance of ignoring the road signs everybody else was following, because I didn't want to go where everybody else was going. In plain English: I didn't want my time to go toward unfulfilling client work. I wanted my time to be devoted to an activity that was much more enjoyable, fulfilling, and meaningful (my filmmaking). But this would probably require a financial sacrifice. And that was why carpooling with my family was so important. They would help me get where I wanted to go by giving me free shelter, thereby lowering my monthly overhead so I wouldn't have to work so much. This is how I'd get the time needed to focus on my filmmaking.

I know it may seem childish and immature, but I was proud of myself. I would never have had the courage to go back to my dad's house if not for my good friend Janüs. Living at my dad's place was luxury compared to the van (no offense, Janüs).

The old Nick would have looked down at the new Nick, but I had grown past the need to be or be seen as an über-independent, successful adult. I'd shed all those external layers — they made me too hot, anyway. I'd been burning up beneath them. So I stripped naked, and all that was left was my bare ass. All you could see was me and only me because there were no more fancy hats to cover up who I truly was. In other words, I was living in alignment with my true self.

* * *

I spent the holidays finishing the financial film series for my client. I even finished my script about a school shooting, entitled *First Person Shooter*, about a bromance gone wrong that proves deadly for the whole student body. After that, 2020 started out with some client work and half a dozen trips. And I still had time to start writing the masterpiece in your hands.

But then, out of the blue, I got a call from a couple of filmmaker friends of mine.

"Are you interested in editing this feature film about quantum physics for us?" They wanted me to carpool with them!

"Uhhhh... yeah!"

I was balls-deep into this work, spending most of my time in the editing room and loving every minute of it, when I started noticing that everybody was wearing masks at the grocery store. Why? I knew it was a bad flu season — I'd even gotten a pretty bad case when I was in San Diego — but why would that scare everybody enough to wear masks at the grocery store? Honestly, I was too busy living the life of my dreams to know what was happening.

Then things started blowing up. There was a global pandemic, then George Floyd, BLM, defund the police, and rioting. Kobe Bryant died, more war in Iran and Iraq, the election, yadda, yadda, yadda... It was like the world had caught on fire (literally, in Australia and California). But this wasn't my reality at all. While everybody else was freaking out, I was thriving. Because I had already decided to live in full alignment with who I was and what my heart truly desired.

It was difficult to be 100-percent me at first — to live at my dad's place, to turn down money, and to effectively take a pay cut. I was heading straight into oncoming traffic, doing things that I had always been told were unacceptable. But, ironically, I was flourishing.

My emotional state on a day-to-day basis was sky-high. My decision had totally paid off. I was living through my heart, and because I was so heart-centric, I was both grounded and heightened at the same time. As a result, the 2020 I experienced was hands-down the best year of my life — the opposite of what was happening globally.

I spent the holidays finishing the financial education film series *How to Save $100K in Your Twenties*, which launched in early 2020 as a full-length feature film. I was told by my client that 25,000 people saw it that year. I was also hired to edit a feature film, *Infinite Potential*, about quantum physicist David Bohm and starring the Dalai Lama, Albert Einstein, and Robert Oppenheimer (50,000 people saw that one). I got a call from a friend of mine who owns a conscious streaming platform called *Conscious Good*, asking if I had any fun projects that she could license. So even a short film I did, *Skylight* — a true story about a stockbroker who comes home one day to find his wife dead in the pool and decides to sell his house and business to start a meditation retreat center in Arkansas — was accepted onto a *paid* streaming platform. All the carpoolers I needed, who were already driving my direction, began showing up.

I followed all this up with a writing retreat on the Oregon coast and finished another feature script just for fun, *Doppelgänger*, about a deadbeat dad who is so jealous of his cooler twin brother that he decides to kidnap him to assume his identity. And I re-released a new cut of my first feature film, *Sharp* — a comedy about a lazy stoner surf-bum who must learn how to sell knives in order to support his family — on Apple TV, Google Play, and Amazon Prime.

I needed other carpoolers, too: I did do some client projects in 2020, but only because they were super cool projects and provided me the gas money I needed to fund my dreams. The rest of my income came from my full-time filmmaking. And I saved more money in 2020 than I had ever saved before.

And finally, it was time to launch the feature documentary I had been working on for six years, *The Miracle Morning*, a documentary on entrepreneurs' morning routines. So, in summer 2020, I drove back to Austin to finish editing a final cut and oversee the finishing touches for a December 2020 release.

I was on the road somewhere in Oregon when I took a phone call with my client (the executive producer of *The Miracle Morning*). He wanted to make some final changes even though we had already locked picture two years earlier. He just knew it could be better, and he wanted to pay me good money to finish it up myself.

We made an agreement, and I hung up the phone.

As I was driving through the middle of nowhere, I became overwhelmed with emotion. I started crying. Weeping, in fact, in pure joy.

Maybe I was releasing years of subconscious pain that I had stuffed deep down inside because I had avoided my gift and lived out of alignment for so long. Or maybe finally realizing my dreams of being a full-time filmmaker was too much to bear. It wasn't that my dreams were coming true; it was the realization that they *had come* true. And it didn't take ten years, as people often say it takes to become an overnight success. It only took a few years of living in a van because I had decided to allow my compass to guide me, turn off my radio, read my own roadmap, ignore the road signs, and floor it toward my dream destination.

* * *

For me, 2020 ended in Austin, Texas, with the live online premiere of my feature documentary *The Miracle Morning* to 7,000 people in twenty-five countries all over the world. And finally, I made a trip back to my hometown of San Diego to visit my mom for the holidays. She had moved into an apartment right down the street from the house I'd lived in with my dad in high school, in a lovely suburban haven called Rancho Bernardo.

Rancho Bernardo was ground zero for me. It was the place where I discovered film and became a filmmaker. Walking along the same trails I had used to get home from school years before, I saw the tree where I had shot my short film about a snail named Melvin. The empty lot that I was kicked out of for trying to shoot a music video was now a fancy retirement community. And the lake that was the location for my first war film was now spanned by a fancy suspension bridge.

Returning to my roots at this juncture of my journey seemed timely. I was able to reflect on how far I had come from a kid playing with a dinky little 3CCD DV video camera out of boredom and curiosity. I wondered what little Nicky would think of adult Nick, now a bona fide filmmaker whose income comes solely from films that impact tens of thousands of people.

For a moment, I actually felt guilty! There I was, in the middle of a global pandemic, while most of the world was panicking because everything was going to shit, and I was having the best year of my life. But it must have been happening to me for some reason.

I had never really believed in luck (the place where opportunity meets preparation). So the reality that manifested for me must have been a result of my choices and actions. I had chosen this destination because of my decision to listen to my mechanics, to steer in the direction of my GPS (my heart), to put my foot on the gas, to face my fears, and to drive myself instead of letting others drive me. It was all because I chose to live life at 70 mph.

I had finally arrived at that seemingly unreachable internal destination: Destination Freedom.

In the beginning, I thought the vanlife would just be something cool to try for a year. I had no idea that it would be so much more than the romantic ideal you see on Instagram.

Vanlife is the way to cleanse. The way to get rid of that which is not serving you. The way to growth. The way to a new you. The way to your own dream destinations.

The van was the vehicle, for me at least, to drive me to my dreams.

And I'm still traveling. Still trucking along. Another destination… Will it never end? Am I just going to keep finding new destinations? When I get to the top of one mountain, I see another peak in the distance, and now I want to go there!

It had taken a few years on the road, but Janüs had done some deep work on me, helping me develop this practice of connecting with my heart's wants and needs, listening carefully to the whispers of my soul, trusting those whispers to guide me.

This whole van thing had created an entirely new life practice. A practice that healed a hole in my heart that I hadn't even been aware of. My GPS directed me not only to destinations of fun and bliss and dreams come true, but also to destinations my heart needed for its own healing.

Destination Freedom isn't some external destination with all the tangible things you've always wanted — career, money, notoriety, a nice house, family… There is no final destination that will solve all your problems. Because the destinations never end. The universe itself is a system of roads that you are navigating.

> To know the universe itself as a road, as many roads, as roads for traveling souls.
>
> —*Walt Whitman, "Song for the Open Road"*

The road of life is endless. So what's the final destination?

When you're lying on your death bed, what will you look back on and appreciate most? It's got to be the road itself, which you're on right now. The journey. It sounds cliché, I know, but that's because it's true. There is no external destination. Destination Freedom is an internal destination.

Now it's your turn to get there by living life at 70 mph.

ABOUT THE AUTHOR

One word: badass.

In past lives, Nick has been a king, a pirate, a samurai warrior, a Buddhist monk, and, most recently, a rock ‘n’ roll star. But this time, he chose to experience planet Earth as an artist.

Guided by lone wolf and jaguar spirits, Nick is here to elevate the consciousness of humanity through the entertaining power of storytelling. His earthly duties include: CEO of Conedera Studios, a six-figure production company creating documentary-style brand films for clients in the personal growth industry, and director of feature films like *SHARP* (2013), *The Miracle Morning* (2020), and *How to Save $100K in Your Twenties* (2020). He has a BFA in Film Production from Chapman University and an MFA in Interdisciplinary Arts from Goddard College.

Nick currently lives in his van, named after the Roman god Janüs, and continues to travel the country.

Made in United States
North Haven, CT
20 October 2021

10455020R00136